MW00777612

Graceful Exits

Graceful Exits

Making the Case for Getting Good at Goodbye

Geri Reid Suster

ROWMAN & LITTLEFIELD
Lanham • Boulder • New York • London

Published by Rowman & Littlefield
An imprint of The Rowman & Littlefield Publishing Group, Inc.
4501 Forbes Boulevard, Suite 200, Lanham, Maryland 20706
www.rowman.com

86-90 Paul Street, London EC2A 4NE

British Library Cataloguing in Publication Information Available

Library of Congress Cataloging-in-Publication Data Available

ISBN 978-1-5381-6930-8 (cloth)
ISBN 978-1-5381-6931-5 (electronic)

This book is dedicated to my gorgeous wolfpack who loved me enough to push me to finish it: Kelly, Beth, Cathy, Penny, Deane, Jo, Sans, Patti, and Terra. Most importantly, to my sons Bar and Jake, for their courage in letting me tell our story and their consistent belief that I can do anything.

Contents

Preface

"Actually, Geri, it's you. We have to let you go." Hearing these words from my dear friend of more than twenty-five years over the phone on a sunny Friday afternoon left me shaking. It was a first for me—being at this end of a layoff. And it was a gut punch.

I experienced the kind of shock that blocks out all other information and focuses the mind like a laser on that exact moment. My thoughts raced through myriad reactions. *Um, excuse me? What do you mean you have to let* me *go? I'm a freaking single mom whose oldest is about to go to college in a few months! Also, you're the one who begged me to leave my previous job eight months ago to come work for you because you had this flipping* great *opportunity! Furthermore, the very reason we are struggling is because* your *sales strategy isn't working. My operations team is ready to go, but since the sales aren't coming, I'm the one being laid off? What the actual fuck?!*

What I learned that day is being laid off is *personal*—no matter how much logic and common sense lie beneath the decision. In the moment when it is happening to us, it is 100 percent personal because it touches on our foundational security and our sense of self-worth, triggering the shame of being singled out from the pack in a negative way. Mind you, as someone with years of management and acquisition experience, I have been on the other side of this layoff scenario more times than I want to admit. However, it wasn't until I experienced it myself that I fully understood how it felt to receive that news.

Okay, here's the deal. It's business and these things happen but . . . ouch. As bad as all of this sounds, the layoff was not the real problem. I was a professional who knew there were risks in moving companies and industries, so although I was reasonably disappointed, I had little justification for being pissed off.

Yet I was really, really pissed off. Livid, in fact. Why? Because my dear friend blindsided me on the phone on a Friday afternoon. Because my access to my staff, the system, and my email was immediately terminated, as though I was some kind of danger to the company. Because, as the chief operating officer, my employment contract guaranteed me thirty days' notice prior to a layoff, which I wasn't given. Because, shortly after this conversation, I found out that my friend and boss actually flew to my location to tell me in person but simply couldn't do it face-to-face and left town instead. And finally, despite my years of service and great results with this individual, I was treated without the dignity and respect I had earned. I simply didn't understand why.

Within days of this experience, I had an epiphany: *life is full of exits.* I made a list of all the exits in my life—jobs, friends, lovers, pets, and experiences. As a manager, I thought of the exits of the employees who worked for me. Some quit, some retired, some were fired, and some were laid off. As I reviewed these many exits, I could see there was a distinct difference in the lingering impact of those exits that were done well and those that were not. Yet when I thought about current practices, I realized that this was an area in which many people really sucked. In our modern society, ghosting is a common part of our dating culture. Businesses conduct massive layoffs via email. Family members die with words left unsaid, of which the COVID-19 pandemic cruelly reminded us.

It doesn't have to be this way.

Don't get me wrong: exiting well is not easy. However, as Glennon Doyle says in her brilliant book *Untamed*, "we can do hard things."[1] Exits happen whether we like it or not, so why not get good at them? How much time did you spend learning to walk, ride a bike, drive a car, or interview for a job? Why not spend a little time learning to approach exits with greater skill? What I know for sure is that an ugly exit—you know, the shocker, the crash-and-burn, or the harsh words you can't take back—not only leaves scars on everyone involved, but adds to the psychological burden one carries long after the exit. On the other hand, a graceful exit is hard in the moment but sets us up to feel lighter and healthier on the other side. If reading this is making you feel uncomfortable, take a deep breath, know that everything is going to be okay . . . and keep reading.

Introduction

> There's a trick to the graceful exit. It means leaving what's over without denying its validity or its past importance to our lives. It involves a sense of future, a belief that every exit is an entry, that we are moving up, rather than out. —Ellen Goodman[1]

"It's *over*," my boss (and dear friend) said. She leaned over my desk, putting her face directly in front of mine. My mind blanked in response to her intense and sudden proclamation. I was confused—what exactly was "over"? Was my job "over"? Was the company "over"? Was there a deal on the table now "over"?

She could see the confusion (and perhaps panic) on my face. She quickly explained: her marriage was, in fact, over. She was seething and electrified, a powerful combination. I, on the other hand, sat there in complete shock. As far as I could tell, there hadn't been any signs. It felt sudden, like when the plane you're flying on suddenly drops several hundred feet in altitude and your stomach relocates to your chest. What could cause something that seemed so solid to apparently disintegrate overnight?

The reason, as it turned out, was as old as time. There was a betrayal. A partner zigged when the other thought the plan was to zag. They took each other for granted, they grew apart, etcetera. The part of the story less examined concerns what happened next—the aftermath of an ungraceful exit. One party became the righteously wronged and the other the dastardly doer. Friends and family picked sides and piled on with the obligatory bashing or defending, while the couple-that-was-no-longer was strapped into a roller coaster of wild emotions that only a sudden change of major life circumstances provides. Unfortunately, this happens all the time.

Shit happens. . . . When one door closes another one opens. . . . Change is the only constant. . . . If you love something, set it free. . . .

Yada, yada, yada! We have dozens of clichés for saying goodbye, when bad things happen, or for unexpected changes in life, yet most of us still don't know how to make a graceful exit. But really, who cares, right? We tell ourselves that we are never going to see that person again after we break up, lay him off, quit our job, or visit her for the last time. It is, after all, an *exit*. The goal is to just walk through that door as quickly as possible and never look back. But I have to ask: How's that been working for you?

An *entrance*, on the other hand, is a different matter entirely. Whether it is walking into a party, starting a new job, going on a first date, or meeting your beloved's eyes at the altar, we tend to give these situations a great deal of thought. Our goal is to make a positive impact. For heaven's sake, there are entire industries built to support this, from improving how we look, how we speak, and how we interview, to how we attract the right mate. Don't even get me started on apps like Pinterest!

What I find interesting is that we rarely strive for a graceful *exit*. In fact, we rarely even think about it except in hindsight. And yet, when a relationship ends suddenly or badly, we wish we had handled our exit better than we ultimately did, because it haunts us for years. Perhaps our optimism or denial gets in the way of considering that an exit is possible, if not likely, to occur in any relationship. Perhaps we are superstitious; if we think about an exit at the beginning, we somehow ensure it will manifest. If we dare to give it thought, whether in business or our personal lives, we tell ourselves that if an end someday occurs, all parties surely will be treated fairly, lovingly, gracefully . . . right?

And yet, we all carry that story, don't we? A love affair gone wrong. Breaking up with someone because we just weren't into it. People laid off. Managers who had to let people go. With each of these exits, real people with a whole host of complex feelings are involved. These exits often are handled poorly, such as when the disruptor drops the bomb and then runs for the hills, leaving the newly disrupted facing a deluge of emotions with no strategy or shelter. The truth is, however, neither party comes away unscathed, as the disruptor is often left with extreme guilt, lowered self-esteem, and anxiety, which can affect how he or she shows up in future relationships.

I propose a better way.

I'm a very logical person. Logic speaks to my need for order, my need to control things, and it helps me make sense of the world. So, I get it: in business and in relationships, it doesn't always work out. There are times when you enter into a relationship with a person or company and despite your best efforts, it isn't a good fit. However, the *way* in which you end a relationship can make all the difference to the collective soul of an organization, to the psyche of an individual, and to the future success of both.

We can do better. I know many people mocked actress Gwyneth Paltrow when she announced her "conscious uncoupling" from her then-husband Chris Martin, but I think she was on to something. I believe she started to change the dialogue about the value of ending a relationship well. Gwyneth's approach was based on Catherine Woodward Thomas's book *Conscious Uncoupling: 5 Steps to Living Happily Even After*. Woodward Thomas defines this type of breakup as being "characterized by a tremendous amount of goodwill, generosity, and respect, where those separating strive to do minimal damage to themselves, to each other, and to their children (if they have any), as well as intentionally seek to create new agreements and structures designed to set everyone up to win, flourish, and thrive moving forward in life."[2]

Sounds good, right? Yet, for those who have been through a difficult exit, this high ideal might seem impossible. The emotions that ride shotgun to most exits can obliterate both reason and empathy.

How do we do better? Ideally, it starts at the beginning. What if we improve the process by setting ground rules at the beginning of our relationships and then, if the worst happens, have the courage to follow through on them? Often, we make it very difficult to find the courage to move through a breakup gracefully because we don't set ground rules. I believe that we can enter into a relationship with a person or a company with eyes wide open and the understanding that we will both do our best. If one or both of us fails, an exit may occur. How we handle that exit is critical in ensuring the success of our next entrance.

For example, if a company doesn't perform, it may not be able to support the individual. This can be due to poor sales, product issues, or economic forces outside of the company's control (hello, Great Recession of 2008 and the ongoing COVID-19 pandemic that began in 2020). Management may have to downsize by a few employees to save the many. If all employees know this is a possibility up front but have a promise of respect from the company in the form of a clear and generous layoff policy, for example, both parties can consciously separate in a way that neither destroys the self-confidence of the laid-off individual nor the reputation of that company. In this world of social media and interconnectedness, every time we fail in this area, we hurt the collective consciousness, not to mention the company's Glassdoor reviews. It doesn't have to be this way.

My personal experience with exits is broad, although by no means at the extreme end of the spectrum (i.e., nurses, addiction counselors, human resources managers, and the Kennedy family). However, it is ample enough to have learned some good stuff along the way. In relationships, I have experienced breakups (a few) and divorce (five among my biological parents and one of my own). In business, I have performed the difficult task of laying off hundreds of people through no fault of their own. I also have watched dozens leave for greener pastures and fired many for poor performance. I have quit a few jobs and have been laid off from one. In life, I have said goodbye to countless pets, a few friends, and, before I turned forty, all my grandparents and parents. Each exit made an impact. There has been a palpable difference between exits that were graceful and those that were not.

With each experience, I learned more about what felt kind or constructive and what felt cruel or unnecessary. My desire was to strive consistently for the former, so I worked diligently to ensure my delivery was attuned to the person receiving the news. I really focused on applying this when I had to lay off someone. When I have been on the other end of that conversation, either in business or personal relationships, my goal has been first to understand and then to act with dignity. I've certainly not been perfect in my execution. However, as one employee told me, I have the gift of being able to tell people that they are not performing while also allowing them to leave the meeting feeling good about themselves.

I wasn't born with this skill and I made several mistakes along the way. At the age of fifteen, I fell in love for the first time with a hunky, smart athlete who was two years older than me. We were together for about a year, during which time I became an unofficial member of his family. It was a sweet time in our lives, but college was approaching for him after graduation, and we knew we were too young to try to keep the relationship going once he went to college. So, we did the sensible thing and decided to break up when he left for school at the end of summer. We had a long, beautiful goodbye, including picnics, flowers, concerts, and tons of memories. Totally graceful.

Had we left it at that, there likely would be no regrets, just wonderful memories and the clear conscience that a graceful exit provides. However, we were young and his university was only thirty minutes away, so there were a few random reunions, which definitely complicated things. Was it just a hookup? Was it more? How did one talk about these things? Clearly, neither of us knew—so we said nothing.

Inevitably, one of us would move on to something more serious—which happened to be me. Because my status with my first love was somewhat gray, I was unsure of how to handle it, so I opted to do and say nothing. When my ex inevitably found out about my new guy, the resulting awkward phone call left me feeling very guilty. A few years later, I ran into him again and received an icy reception. To this day, a small ache is tucked into a corner of my heart due to the way I handled this exit. I regret that I did not communicate more and strive for clarity in our status *before* I moved on, since I never wanted to cause this man pain. Contrary to popular culture, the one who is dumped is not the only one who hurts after a breakup. I have found that guilt and regret can be just as painful as rejection . . . and may even last longer.

I also have learned something else: *the pain you cause becomes the pain you carry*.

Witnessing the different outcomes between graceful and ungraceful exits inspired me to write this book. Facing change is a skill, and a graceful exit is about more than simply surviving the change. *It is about coming out whole on the other side*. Imagine a world where we possessed the skills to end relationships without feeling horrible because we showed up with integrity, created space for the other person's pain, and grieved with them. Ultimately, it is about coming out with gratitude for the experience and love for those no longer in your life.

Sound crazy? Let me show you how to handle exits better and more gracefully in relationships, at work, and in life.

Part I

PERSONAL

I know for sure that love saves me and that it is here to save us all.
—Maya Angelou[1]

If we are lucky, personal relationships comprise an enormous portion of our lives, from parents, guardians, siblings, friends, relatives, bosses, employees, coworkers, pets, and lovers. How we interact with others is usually guided by how we were raised, what we observe in others, and whom we admire. Yet very little formal training is provided regarding how to be good at personal relationships in the normal course of life, so we are often left to figure it out as we go along. I recall much trial and error at the dinner table—with corrections from my parents or teasing from my older siblings—if I blurted something they deemed inappropriate.

At elementary school, I reenacted these unwritten social rules on the playground, only to find that not everyone followed the same playbook. Often those in authority, such as teachers, provided guidance based on how they were taught. I also noticed that my friends who belonged to formal religions or spiritual belief systems received more consistent and specific instructions about what to consider "right" and "wrong." At the end of the day, most of us were left with some vague guiding principles, such as "be nice," "do unto others as you would have them do unto you," "do the right thing," etcetera. Consequently, we emerge as adults with ideas about how to treat each other, but not necessarily with a great deal of skill in executing these concepts.

Therefore, it is not surprising that when a personal relationship must change, one or both parties often handles it poorly. The goal of a graceful exit in relationships is to combine a logical approach with an environment that leaves space for emotions. The end of a personal relationship can be traumatic and cause lasting scars that impact future relationships. In order to avoid that scarring, we tend to try to exit quickly. Often, that scars us the most. In fact, sudden exits in our personal lives are among the most traumatic, because the underlying expectation tends to be that you will be family/friends/lovers/spouses *forever*.

Speaking of trauma, it's important to understand the psychological concept of big T (*Trauma*) and little T (*trauma*). Big T includes life-threatening situations such as combat, natural disasters, and physical and sexual abuse. It can be associated with post-traumatic stress syndrome. Little T is created by distressing events that cause harm but are not immediately life threatening. Examples of little Ts include loss of a loved one, a bad breakup, loss of a job, and emotional abuse. However, a combination of little Ts or repeated exposure to them can cause more emotional harm than experiencing a big trauma. In other words, trauma can be compounded, which reminds me of the phrase "adding insult to injury." We need to recognize that the loss of a primary relationship is a form of trauma. If we handle it with grace, we can avoid piling on additional trauma—freeing both parties to enjoy better future relationships.

Additionally, every individual's personal trauma history is unique. It is important to consider this when engaging with others. What you might consider "not a big deal" could be the tipping point into depression and self-loathing for another. Taking time to consider that before communicating an exit is important. Also, by leaving space for the possibility that you might get a bigger reaction than what seems "reasonable," you can create an exit plan with greater empathy and less unintentional cruelty.

We know on a general level that friendships fade, breakups happen, and life is finite. We also know there is trauma in the world. And yet, most people don't think it will happen to us, to *this* friendship or *this* marriage or *this* loved one. Ironic, right? Such denial can create some painful and unnecessary consequences in our lives. Let's take a look at some examples.

Chapter One

What's Our Friends-
and-Family Plan?

It is easy to love the people far away. It is not always easy to love those close to us. —Mother Teresa[1]

They say family is forever and friends are the family we choose, so how do we let go of friends when they no longer seem to fit in our life? Do we stop returning calls or make excuses? How do we know when we have been released? How hard do we push to revive a faded friendship? In order to feel clean about a change in friendship, whether leaving a friend behind or being left behind, *it is important to know the reason.* The imagination is a powerful thing. It amplifies our emotional or psychological state. Without a reason for the change, we often make up stories that are much worse than reality.

THE FAIL

Let me give you an example from my own life in which I really screwed things up unnecessarily. I have a dear friend, whom I will call Meg, that I have known since high school. She never harmed me in any way. She was a true and loyal friend from the moment I met her. As we grew older, got married, and had kids, we saw each other less frequently but stayed in touch. When I moved back to my hometown where Meg still lived, I was able to see her more often. Our families would hang out from time to time and we got to know each other as adults and parents.

During this time, I experienced some serious spiritual and emotional growth. As a result, I began to find that some of Meg's behavior (toward herself) bothered me. It reminded me of a painful dysfunctional family dynamic, and I could no longer be around her without getting upset. This was through no fault of her own, as she had not changed. However, I had. Rather than telling Meg this, I avoided her, which was difficult because she lived close to me. I avoided her because I thought I would come across as judging her choices, which was not my place to do. I never gave her any kind of feedback; I just dropped out of her life.

Meg reached out occasionally; I did not respond. She sent greeting cards; I did not answer them. I was being a flat-out crappy friend by ghosting her. I simply could not find the courage or words to share my feelings for fear of offending her, yet my behavior of dropping out of her life was surely offensive. See how my "good intentions" were harmful? Meanwhile, I lived with low-grade, ever-present guilt because of this. My guilt spiked whenever I drove near her street or saw her kids walking to school. Clearly, I was creating damage and pain for everyone involved. I had to ask myself, *so how is this easier than being honest?*

THE BETTER WAY

Eventually, I could no longer live with my lack of integrity in this relationship. Avoiding a tough conversation was not worth the guilt I felt. I made understanding my emotions a top priority and, with the help of my favorite therapist, gained clarity about my feelings.

I asked Meg to coffee and explained my behavior. I shared that I had changed and that her behavior was triggering me because of work I was doing on my past. I also shared how unfair it was to withhold this information for so long, but I just hadn't understood it completely myself. I explained that she had not changed and she had always been a great and loyal friend. Then I apologized—sincerely and deeply.

Immense relief washed over her when she realized it was about me and not about something she had done. I felt terrible for putting her through this and for causing her to think she had done something wrong. Had I been honest with myself from the beginning and prioritized doing my internal work to identify my reason for exiting, I would have greatly reduced the amount of pain and guilt we both experienced.

This brings us to one of the key ingredients of a graceful exit: asking the question, *why?* Why is this exit happening? With Meg, it took me some time to work through the "why" and then to find the courage to share it with her. That delay caused unnecessary pain for both of us.

PREVENTION

The easiest way to prevent misunderstandings is to work hard to maintain healthy and expanding relationships with everyone in your life. This is similar to tending a garden, in that you must be diligent about and find pleasure in the maintenance to enjoy a consistent and abundant harvest. However, that does not ensure that individuals won't grow in different directions. People with whom I was close in high school now live lifestyles very different and incompatible with mine. This happens throughout the various stages of our lives and is completely normal.

However, there is a way to prevent pain when this happens—by practicing honest and compassionate communication. Had I shared more of my personal growth story with Meg, we both likely would have held a greater understanding of the changing dynamics in our friendship. We would have naturally shifted in our friendship together so that no one was left behind wondering while the other was feeling guilty. If you are aware of the health of the relationship as it unfolds, there are fewer surprises.

Remember, the goal is not to communicate in order to change the other person's mind or behavior. The goal is to understand where the other stands in real time with regard to the relationship. The only way to do this is through ongoing, honest, and intimate communication. Have coffee regularly or schedule a monthly hike. Give yourself the time to stay in touch. If this is happening and either party begins to grow in a new direction, it will be observed and discussed openly. If differences become too great, the relationship may fade, but it will likely be a conscious, guilt-free transition.

What about that friend with whom great stretches of time pass without talking, and then when we reconnect, we pick back up like no time has passed? Nearly all of us have someone like that in our lives. I suggest we recognize that for what it is—a freaking blessing. You and that person are truly compatible. However, that does not mean all your other relationships can and should be the same. If you happen to enjoy one that appears effortless, cherish that gorgeous being even more. You might even find folks with whom you had little in common earlier in life growing into your kind of people (or you have grown into theirs). By embracing all possibilities, you remain open to being pleasantly surprised by life.

Speaking of surprises, some exits come out of nowhere. The shock of the sudden loss can take our breath away (among other things). However, we can see other exits coming for years, such as the death of an aging parent or a child's transition to adulthood. Unfortunately, that does not always make it easier, which is why another key ingredient to creating a graceful exit is *acceptance that the exit is going to happen.* Often, so much precious time and energy is wasted in denial and we miss the little moments when the universe signals change in bite-sized chunks. If we stay in the present moment during the process and allow ourselves to feel as we go, we will acclimate to the new normal as it's happening. A great example of this is when children grow up and fly out of the family nest—another major life exit.

Let's dig into this.

THE FAIL

Parenting is both the hardest and most rewarding job in the world. Literally. The pressure to get it right is intense, and yet mistakes are guaranteed. Every child is unique and goes through so many stages in the first five years alone it is no wonder that keeping up as a parent is so hard. Yet, however quickly time goes by (and it does), every parent knows (or should know) that someday, if you are lucky, the child will leave. It is actually in the job description—raising this being from infant to adult. That said, *many* parents have a surprisingly difficult time letting go of their offspring. I know several parents that have experienced this to an extreme. As a parent myself, let me tell you that the struggle is real.

One of the worst examples I have seen firsthand is the mom of one of my son's classmates. I will call her Lucy. Lucy is a great mom who stays at home with her four kids and is involved in everything they do. She volunteers, drives, and chaperones all events. She considers her kids her "best friends." She posts about them frequently on social media—from what she makes them for breakfast to the results of each athletic endeavor.

When her eldest child prepared for college, Lucy lamented—frequently. When her child left, she was inconsolable. She visited at college often and rejoiced at each homecoming, only to lament again each time her child returned to school. The following year, when her second child left for college, the process began again. I wondered about the impact her reaction made on each of her children. Mom's love might have been flattering to the children initially, but I wondered if it became a burden to them at some point. Did they feel guilty that their parent was so upset? Did the siblings feel concern? Did they consider changing their future plans to avoid the same reaction? Did her husband feel concerned or slighted in any way?

As I reflected on this dynamic, I realized that Lucy had made her children her life—literally. The tasks and events in their daily lives were her tasks and events. Everything she did was about those kids. Although this behavior is admirable to an extent, Lucy missed the fork in the road during their adolescence, her opportunity to begin letting go.

The minute your child—or her best friend—gets a driver's license, she is often gone. Rather than following her, stalking her, or asking to join her, this is your opportunity to get reacquainted with yourself. Easier said than done, I know, but just like potty training, it has to happen sometime. The longer you wait, the more awkward it becomes.

THE BETTER WAY

When it was time for my firstborn son, Bar, to leave for college, I experienced much of the same angst as any parent. He had grown up too fast and I worried that I had forgotten to teach him something or to prepare him for the endless challenges of daily life. However, I was thrilled for the experience and adventure I knew he would have, and that joy carried me through the other stuff. My years of therapy taught me to process emotions as they happened and to live more fully in the now. Without this therapy, I likely would have ended up like my friend Lucy.

When I visited my son's college for orientation, it hit me that he would soon be moving out of my home. Rather than pushing the thought away, I tried to embrace it by processing what I was feeling in that moment. I stepped away from the campus tour and found a peaceful spot to journal. Here is my entry:

> I am here on this campus that will be my son's new home. It's difficult to think of him having a home other than mine but it's exciting at the same time. As I sit looking across this beautiful green quad, it's as if I am trying to soak up all of the molecules in the space—breathe it all in—to ensure that I have a piece of his new home with me—as though that is a link we will share when I miss him.

Once I was back home and walked by his empty room, I felt a powerful twinge of loss. Back to the journal I went:

> This morning I wake up in my home with one less child in my house and I am swirling with strange mixed emotions. I feel worry and pride and love and some relief—some sense of accomplishment—feeling lighter that my responsibility as a parent has been fulfilled to a certain degree. I have passed a major milestone of some sort on my journey and it is such a blessing as this journey, with this being, has been amazing and probably one of the greatest experiences in my life. And now he is gone and out of my nest and ready—a great human being. I am so grateful that I was able to accomplish this objective—this dream of mine and that he met me halfway, more than halfway and we worked together to get him from baby to man. It's a beautiful partnership and I'm really proud of it. And as I sit here in my front room, I see a beautiful hummingbird—a symbol of joy—and I must remember that while I will miss him and I will worry, it is nothing but a privilege and a joy to have your son go off to college and that on this day, there is much to rejoice.
>
> In terms of leaving your son in another state at college, the thing that made me feel better was getting his room set up, getting his supplies, making sure he had his books, making sure he knew how to get food. And then at some point, he was ready for us to go and it was kind of the signal that I needed that it was okay. Hugs and pictures and then . . . on the road. I thought I would be more devastated. I was more worried leading up to it rather than driving away. But it is only day one. Technology helps. I am grateful for intuitive guidance leading up to this exit, embracing the change, feeling it and considering the best possible path to the inevitable. One of the things about preparing for the change that helped was explaining to my son what this meant to me—what my possible reactions would be and that they really had nothing to do with him. I just kind of warned him as I started to have these feelings and I felt myself putting

great importance on these events that had more to do with my childhood and my hopes and dreams back when I was his age than it did with him.

A few nights before he left, we had a beautiful moment when he was talking about trying to come home for something relatively soon into the process and I said I think you should stay there and immerse yourself in your new environment. I started to get stressed out because I was afraid he was not going to be fully engaged, which were my fears being projected on him. And he had the sense and maturity to say to me, "Mom, I don't want to argue with you about this right now." And it stopped me in my tracks and he said it with such maturity and just set the boundary and I just said, right on. I'm going to bed now and he said goodnight, love you—I said I love you too. It was all very positive, not an argument, just beautiful. I thought, he's got it; he's mature and kind. I am blessed. I thank God for this experience and there are so many more to come. I thank God I got to be his mother—best job in the world for me.

As it turned out, he decided to stay at school during the weekend in question on his own. We came up with a system in which we talked on the phone about once a week, with random "you alive?" texts in between. Our calls became long and rich with stories and laughter— pure joy. Did I miss him? Of course! Yet with each week that went by, we both gained confidence in his ability to navigate his new life. He learned to budget and do his own laundry. He got sick and hurt but then leaned on his new friends to help him get to urgent care and the hospital when needed. As a result, he survived, made lifelong friends, and developed a whole new appreciation for his mom.

When he came home for visits, our relationship was different. He pitched in and I moved from mom to more of a mentor/cheerleader role. I helped only when asked, and sometimes, I declined. Because of how we worked through his exit together, there was no guilt or resentment between us. As a result, our relationship became stronger. I am very proud of this transition because there was a time, years ago, when I didn't think I would ever be able to let him go.

PREVENTION

There is a saying that motherhood is about letting your heart walk around outside of your body (in the form of your children), so it is no wonder that letting go is so difficult. From the moment they are pulled from your body, these little beings are all about growing and learning to become independent. Therefore it is important to look at parenting as a series of transitions from dependence to independence. First you stop nursing, then they begin to feed themselves, move themselves from point A to point B, learn to talk, and begin sharing their opinions (i.e., "No!"). Then they go to school, make new friends, graduate to the next grade, to middle and high school. Then they begin driving. That's when you know they are really taking off. When they reach adulthood, they are suddenly "independent" in the eyes of the law. You begin to see their life take shape (and your role change from main character to a supporting character). It's quite a ride!

I believe that the key to letting a child go begins by getting comfortable with letting him grow. If you find you don't want to stop nursing, co-sleeping, or carrying your child despite his or her straining for independence, then perhaps you are having trouble letting go and allowing your child to move to the next stage. Many children's health experts suggest that children often indicate when they are ready to climb the next hill. If we are the ones ignoring those signals, we might want to do some soul searching with ourselves or our partner. *But how do I let go when I love them so much and it is my job to protect them?* I get it, from a genuine been-there, done-that perspective. In my experience, the only salve to this wound is savoring each moment of each stage as much as you can. Photograph it if you must.

In elementary school, progress milestones are everything. Teachers, those glorious creatures, send home amazing and creative proof that your child knows her colors, was kind to a classmate, can count to ten, and at some point (*thank you, Jesus!*) completed her multiplication tables. It was easier then to stay present with our child's growth and progression. Milestones were celebrated and all kinds of stuff pasted to the fridge.

In middle school, that changed. The feedback became more mature, in the form of report cards. Upon reflection, this would have been a great moment for me to take over tracking their progression, but as any parent of a middle schooler will tell you, you are likely hanging on for dear life amid the hormones and social pressures. At some point— perhaps because I missed or felt nostalgic for elementary school—we started doing a casual annual inventory to look back at all we had done the previous year and what we still wanted to do as individuals and as a family. This helped with showing our progress and kept me more in touch with the passage of time. By trying to stay present with our children, we will not feel as though we have missed anything and will more readily notice the signs when our children are ready for growth.

Additionally, talk to your child about upcoming milestones so that everyone knows what to expect. This tends to happen naturally, but sometimes we forget to discuss little steps, like when they can walk to school by themselves, when they can have their first sleepover, when they can begin dating, or when they can get their first cell phone. It's important to have a game plan for these milestones with your partner in parenting (if you have one) so that you are not blindsided one day by your child with a request for which you have not prepared. Also, by planning ahead, you are mentally preparing yourself for the next stage well before it smacks you in the face.

In many cultures and religious practices, there are rites of passage: rituals to mark the transition from childhood to adulthood. My family never participated in such rituals when I was growing up. But when a friend who also has two sons told me she was doing a "becoming a man" trip with her eldest, I fell in love with the idea. When my firstborn turned twelve, I took him to New York City—just the two of us. It was magical. He lit up in the city. My shy, quiet boy came alive; by the second day, he was hailing cabs like a native.

When my youngest, Jake, turned twelve, we went to San Francisco for his rite of passage trip. We explored the hills, Chinatown, and rode Segways through Golden Gate Park. On both trips, we visited art galleries and took in live theater. These were big investment trips, and I was fortunate to be able to afford them, but the same could be accomplished with a camping trip or hiking adventure. The idea is to do something you have never done before, something that is a bit of a stretch. It is a perfect time to acknowledge that they have matured and to renegotiate both freedoms and responsibilities. You get the idea.

Now I'm not saying that a rite-of-passage trip magically eliminates the pain of letting go of your child. However, I *am* saying that it might keep you out of denial and allow you to celebrate little milestones along the way rather than dreading them—or even worse, ignoring them. Also, I recommend visualizing your child as a strong, independent adult with a job and an apartment, learning to budget and pay bills. You might even start a trunk when your child is young and add to it until he moves to a place of his own. In it, put family photos, kitchenware, linens, and so forth so that he has a starting point and knows that you have been planning for this day for some time. Then give it to them.

Remember, there is no greater evidence of a well-raised child than a young adult able to successfully stand on his own.

Chapter Two

When Nuclear Goes Boom

Never cut what can be untied. —Portuguese proverb

Ahh, romance. It is fraught with both angst and delicious emotion. As such, we often choose, pivot, and decide from a place of emotion rather than logic. We are taught from an early age that romantic relationships should be magical fairy tales full of chivalry, dancing, and proclamations of love that make the coldest hearts swoon. Social media, with its never-ending highlight reel of perfect relationship moments, has taken the fantasy to the next level with no signs of stopping. I mean, have you seen the "promposals"? Those create big expectations. What could possibly go wrong?

In his book *Your Brain at Work*, Dr. David Rock discusses the impact that expectations have on one's happiness. "Expectations are also central in the creation of upward and downward spirals in the brain. They can take you to the peak of performance, or to the depths of despair. Maintaining the right expectations in life may be central for maintaining a general feeling of happiness and well-being."[1] In other words, having unrealistic expectations going into any relationship is akin to stepping onto a minefield.

Few of us are taught what to look for in a spouse. The only advice I received from my mom that I can recall is that I definitely should have sex *before* getting married to make sure we are compatible in that area. Clearly, this related to her personal history. I recall feeling that it was too much information at the time. As such, I chose my first husband based on my feelings: my big, dramatic, raised-in-a-dysfunctional-household feelings. I gave zero thought to our long-term compatibility, as evidenced by the fact that he is, at heart, a conservative, gun-loving hunter of animals while I am a liberal, don't-want-guns-in-my-house animal lover. I see it now, as obvious as the nose on my face. Then, I was under the influence and not using my brain.

Which leads to a logical question: *Okay, Geri, not all marriages fail, so what do you attribute that to?* Hmmm . . . how about luck? Seriously, there are people that choose well either as a result of a functional childhood anchored and modeled by their parents' good marriage or some inner guidance system that I clearly did not possess. I also believe that premarital counseling is a critical step to ensure marital success. According to Rachel Kleinman of YourTango.com, "80 percent of experts polled agree that couples who attend premarital education/counseling are less likely to get divorced than couples who don't."[2]

But what about those of us who never got the memo before we dove in with our raging emotions? Are we just failures? Or is there some greater reason or purpose to our adventures in love? On a more spiritual plane, I know every relationship in my life brought opportunities to learn, grow, and even heal from things in my past. Sometimes that means growing in the same direction and sometimes that means growing apart and starting anew.

So let's dive deeper into how wrong it can go.

THE FAIL

I met my now ex-husband when I was nineteen and he was twenty-five. My initial instincts? *To run in the opposite direction!* He wasn't my type and his interests were totally different than mine. Plus, he seemed a little too charming. Yet he was persistent. After many weeks of that full-wattage charm and during a moment of weakness (I was half asleep at the time), I agreed to go out with him.

Our first date ended up being fun, but I was still guarded. After several more dates, I was in the same boat—I enjoyed the time we spent together and peeking into his world, but deep down I felt hesitation. Then he took me to a motorcycle race, something about which he was passionate, and I was able to see his best self. He was so excited to share this with me and took the time to explain everything. It was a magical night and I fell under the influence. From that point forward, I completely ignored the previous weeks of hesitation in which my inner guidance system was pumping the brakes. I threw caution to the wind and we became inseparable.

Don't get me wrong: we had a ton of fun and romance and adventure. I learned new things, went to new places, and met new people. It was lovely—until it wasn't. It turns out we were incompatible on a few key issues, such as having children, money management, political party affiliation, gun ownership, and international travel. But we were in love! Ultimately, I was too young to know what I wanted, so there was no way I could know if we wanted the same things. A classic rookie mistake.

During our four-year courtship, we broke up a couple of times but always found our way back to that old, comfortable pattern partially rooted in our mutual childhood dysfunction. We both ignored the signs of our incompatibility and did the only logical next thing: we got married!

Two moves and two sweet children later, it all came crashing down in a dramatic blaze of glory.

Before getting to the ungraceful exit, I feel the need to share the key things that led up to it. First, I had been fortunate to work for an amazing company with a great deal of growth opportunity and financial stability. My career was taking off. However, my ex worked in a less stable industry and often changed jobs as a result. This could be highly frustrating for both of us. Additionally, about three years into our marriage, I realized that I wanted children. Up until that point, I hadn't been sure, but after some soul searching I realized the future I saw for myself definitely included rug rats. So I veered off course from the girl he first met and how our lives worked up until that point. After much discussion, he agreed to join me in the adventure called parenting.

When we had our first child, I changed again. Once I became a mother, my priorities shifted, and I assumed his would as well. He seemed to approach parenting differently in that he thought having a child wouldn't change our lives. We would just add another body into the mix, right? We were at different ends of the parenting spectrum, and the more I pushed for my end, the more he pulled for his. Adding our second child did nothing to lessen this conflict, and soon my ex was straining for his old life. First, he started racing motorcycles again, then he bought a boat, then a big truck, then a bigger boat. You get the picture. The incompatibility in our priorities caused my resentment to build toward him. Our relationship suffered. The boys were our only true joy in our day-to-day living—the small moments that made everything else less important. This carried us through our days and gave me the sense that it would all be okay.

When the boys were eight and five years old, my mom, my best friend at the time, was diagnosed with stage 4 lung cancer and given six months to live. I changed again. In addition to working full time and handling most parenting and household duties, I was now a part of my mom's triage team. Weekly communication to our extended family and a huge group of friends took up what little extra time and focus I had. Updates from my stepfather and sister and my mom's doctor appointments were squeezed into my schedule. My husband, who preferred to run from this situation, was squeezed out.

As the months flew by, I could feel both my husband and my mom slipping away from me. I assumed, incorrectly as it turned out, that my husband was avoiding facing my mom's illness and possible death because they were close and he just couldn't handle it. Although that might have been part of it, it wasn't all of it—as I would later discover.

On the last Friday in August 2004, my sweet, funny, strong, beautiful, artistic mother passed away. Three days later, on the following Monday, I discovered that my fourteen-year marriage was over as well. It was the first day of school for my kindergartener and third grader. Because of those amazing children, I will not get into the gory details. Suffice it to say, my husband had fallen in love with someone else and I found out by chance. The exit had been happening, and I was too busy with the many other things going on in my life to notice.

After intense discussions with him during the next couple of days, we both knew that it was over. Two weeks later, my family hosted my mom's celebration of life, at which I spoke in front of hundreds of people—without my husband by my side. He was busy moving out of our home that day.

This type of exit was *brutal*. First, there was the failure of the relationship and loss of my partner and friend, along with the beautiful dreams I had for our future together. This alone was a large pill to swallow. However, my grief was compounded by the fact that I had been immediately replaced, so I now waded through betrayal on top of loss. In a three-day span, my sense of who I was in the world was so badly damaged that I had no other choice but to shut down my heart and live in my head until further notice.

Looking back, I can say definitively that the betrayal was much worse than my husband choosing to leave due to general incompatibility. I attribute this to the selfish nature of betrayal, because it is the result of a hurtful choice made by someone you once trusted.

It was the most intense period of my life. I was thirty-eight years old and not sure how to deal with everything that was coming at me, so I went into survival mode. I shut off almost all emotion and focused on the tasks that needed to be done: plan the service, find a therapist, find a mediator so I could file for divorce, take my kids to school, go to work (kind of), respond to the outpouring of love from all over, tell my family and friends about my ending marriage, go to mediation, go to therapy to find out how to tell my kids what was happening, and so on. I was a machine running on pure adrenaline for at least a month.

The single worst moment in that period (and my life) was telling my two sweet boys with my soon-to-be ex that "mommy and daddy are getting a divorce." What a crushing and brutally horrible blow to deliver to these children. It rips my heart out whenever I think about that moment, because a parent's job is to protect their children from harm. Yet here we were, causing it. No matter how much you whitewash it, divorce hurts children, robbing them of some level of innocence and security. You may tell yourself that you are all better off living in a peaceful home or having two birthdays or whatever drivel you want to use to justify it, but that is denial and self-preservation. So think long and hard before getting married, having kids, and deciding to walk away. More importantly, you owe it to yourself and your future children to take all steps necessary to prevent this. But I digress. . . .

It is important to know, which I cannot stress enough, that the aftermath of this type of exit can be especially brutal for the one who is exiting. In this case, my husband became the worst kind of villain in the hearts and minds of family and friends. I heard comments like, "he was doing that while your mother was dying?" and "oh, your poor children." People rushed to my side, spewing angry insults about him to me out of loyalty or in an effort to empathize with me in some way. Part of me wanted and needed to hear it (let's be honest), but part of me felt worse, considering they were talking about the man I chose to marry and the father of my children. What did that say about us?

The desire to hate my ex in order to come to terms with the loss of my marriage was strong, but I quickly gave warning to family and friends that although I appreciated the support, no one was to say anything negative about my ex to my kids. Prior to the implosion of my life, I was fortunate to read something that explained that children see themselves as half of each parent, so when one parent speaks poorly of the other, the child believes that he or she must be bad as well. Because of this nugget from the universe, my mission became to leave the venting to visits with friends over wine and away from my kids.

Meanwhile, my ex also went through an extremely difficult period. His family and friends either withdrew from him or were very critical of him. He also was grieving the loss of my mother but was not allowed to express it because of his actions. He did not attend her service and could not hang out with her husband, one of his dear friends, to help him through the process. He was cast out and left to build a new life while saddled with a ton of grief and guilt. Not so pretty on that side either, right? When the exit is not graceful, friends and family often feel the need to choose sides, which extends the problem out into the world.

More than a decade later, I asked my ex to lunch to inform him that I was writing this book and that our story would be included. Before I got to that, I asked him if he ever thought about how he handled his exit. "I think about it every day," he responded immediately. I was surprised—not that he thought about it, but that he thought about it so often and then responded without hesitation. The fact that it had weighed him down for more than five thousand days (by my calculation) was incredibly sad.

As we continued our lunch, I shared my plans to publish this book. Half-joking, he immediately said, "Oh man, that's not gonna be good for me." When I further explained that my position was one of empathy for all that he went through, he seemed stunned. He then came to understand my belief that we are not taught the skills to create graceful exits and that I was hoping our story might help others do better in the future in a multitude of settings. He seemed relieved and inspired. We walked away from that lunch feeling both closer and lighter.

THE BETTER WAY

The reason for the ungraceful ending of my marriage was due to both how and when it happened. Cheating is not a graceful exit strategy, nor is falling in love with someone else while committed to another. But it happens so often that I'm convinced we do not have the tools to avoid it. In this scenario, the more graceful alternative is straightforward.

When my husband or I started to see that our marriage was in trouble, we should have talked about it. One of us should have had the courage to bring it up, and both of us should have had the courage to seek counseling. By developing some measure of self-awareness through counseling, we could begin to own our missteps. I'm not saying this would have saved the marriage, but it might have. Even if it didn't, then the exit would be one we both saw coming and could more easily accept because we both had tried our best to make it work. It would have given us some time to work through the slew of difficult emotions surrounding a failed marriage before having to inform our children. This would have allowed us to present a unified front to them and to develop a game plan.

However, neither of us were that self-aware. When my husband started feeling attraction toward someone else, he should have discussed it with me or gone to see a counselor. Attraction that makes you want to act is obviously a major red flag to your relationship and the most critical moment to seek counsel. We each have oodles of buttons and baggage accumulated throughout our lives, and temptation to do the wrong thing almost always arises from one of these. Achieving some level of self-awareness is a major advantage in helping us find grace in our choices.

Although they received some criticism for it, I greatly admire Gwyneth Paltrow and Chris Martin, who were brave enough to change the dialogue around divorce and how it is supposed to go. We have seen the couple co-parent successfully, move on to dating without huge amounts of drama, and even take family vacations together. I'm sure it wasn't all drama free, but it appears to be much better than what so many of us experience. That's a graceful exit.

This work is worth the effort for no other reason than what it means for your future, says Woodward Thomas: "bad breakups caused people to live diminished lives as much as twenty years later."[3]

All one needs to do to understand the profound truth of Woodward Thomas's statement is to witness a bad divorce. If you have no such experience, congratulations! Now, go stream the following movies for your education: *Kramer vs. Kramer*, *War of the Roses*, and *Marriage Story*. There is truth in those gut-wrenching depictions. On top of that, the average divorce takes about eleven months to finalize—eighteen months if it goes to trial. When major assets and/or custody is in question, divorce often takes longer and gets uglier. Going for a more graceful exit isn't just nicer, it's also smarter.

Rituals are another option to consider when attempting to navigate a graceful exit. In Japan at the Mantokuji temple in Gunma, there is a "divorce toilet" where you can flush your failed marriage away. The intention is to rid yourself of bad relationship karma by writing breakup wishes on paper and flushing them down the toilet. Although there is something funny about this, there is also something powerful. Rituals help move individuals through the grieving process, without which they may remain stuck in a place of pain and anger. Instead of using a toilet, you could use fire and a full moon to release your written wishes.

One of my favorite rituals, a "ceremony of hope," is provided by the Universal Unitarian Church, which has a loving and accepting culture around divorce. Its website states the following regarding divorce rites:

> For many reasons, a marriage falls short of expectation. The days are cold. The nights are long. Again and again. The marriage partners try to recapture the dream they had; to live the vision they both once believed. Yet the marriage is broken. It is a struggle of impossibility. All too often, confronted by society's uncomprehending disapproval, the other's disappointment and resentment, and one's own specters of failure and inadequacy, the choice must be made to walk alone. Paths must part. (Rev. Rudolph Nemser)
>
> When people marry, they make vows to each other. When the marriage ends, it is emotionally helpful and healing to be released from such vows and to begin again in a spirit of compassion, forgiveness, and hopefulness.[4]

Similar to a wedding, the ceremony takes place in the church among close family and friends. The former couple stands before these witnesses to acknowledge any pain or disappointment caused in the marriage and to seek mutual forgiveness. Although there is recognition of marital difficulties during the ceremony, much of the content is geared toward hope and moving forward peacefully. As the church's divorce rites state:

> [the] minister reminds them that they were married within the community, and that the community is now present for their divorce. The individuals are then led in an affirmation that, though their marriage is ending, they will endeavor to value the past and enter a new, respectful relationship that transcends the pain and bitterness of the recent past.[5]

There is no designated timeline for when this ceremony occurs—simply when the couple is ready.

Rituals and ceremonies are great tools for helping one or both parties move through the many emotional stages of breaking up. The key is listening to what you need and having the patience with your soon-to-be ex to accommodate what he or she needs. Creating grace requires courage from both parties. Partners who leave must have the courage to be honest and hold space for the pain they create. The ones being left must bravely face the change being forced upon them while also acknowledging their own roles in the failure of the relationship. No matter how right or wrong one party might seem at the time of the breakup, both parties usually contribute to its demise. As time passes, it is important for one's own personal growth, healing, and success in future relationships to do this type of inventory because, as Katherine Woodward Thomas says, "Your next relationship doesn't begin when you meet your next lover; it begins with how you ended your last relationship."[6]

PREVENTION

Preventing a failed romance begins with a couple of things: knowing yourself and knowing what you want in a partner. In the extremely helpful book *Be Your Own Dating Service*, author Nina Atwood suggests that in a relationship, each individual should know their own "nonnegotiables," which she calls "building blocks for compatibility,"[7] *before* picking a partner. She cites some of the following examples as possible nonnegotiables:[8]

- Nonsmoker
- Very light drinker; drug free

- Treats animals and children with kindness
- Respects and supports my work
- Stays present to deal with conflict; lives in the same city
- Not verbally or physically abusive
- Committed to personal growth

You get the idea. Some of these are obvious and some not as much, but the point is to decide on your own list of must-haves based on your personal values. Additional and important nonnegotiables worth consideration include whether or not you want children, the importance of and your expectations around religious beliefs, and your financial philosophy regarding risk versus security. As Atwood states, "These are things that, if we compromise on them, will cause us to lose a very basic part of ourselves. Nonnegotiables are the building blocks of compatibility in a relationship, without which all the love, chemistry, and great packaging in the world will be useless."[9] Kind of important, right?

Try to create a list early and revisit it often. Parents should introduce this concept to their children at an appropriate age and guide them in developing a strong sense of what they would like in a partner and why. Parents can also discuss how they picked their own spouses and what traits they admire in the other by way of example. Most importantly, however, parents should do all of this *before* their children begin dating and fall "under the influence." This type of exercise teaches young minds to be discerning while counteracting the fairy-tale bullshit we are often fed by the entertainment industry. Don't get me wrong, I like fantasy as much as the next person, but it took me a while to recognize it as fantasy. By that time, I had already kissed too many frogs. With such a list, the chances of your significant other meeting much of your criteria increases dramatically when you fall in love.

In addition to the nonnegotiable list, Atwood suggests that we also compile a negotiables list. This includes physical traits (i.e., tall, dark, and handsome) or hobbies (likes to cook). These are nice to have, not must-haves. Depending upon your personal priorities, they may affect chemistry and compatibility. Once dating has commenced, the goal is to compare your list against theirs to determine if you are a true match (before you fall under the influence).

Once that first hurdle has been cleared, the couple should join forces to develop a set of expectations (like a mission statement) for their relationship. How will you handle conflict? How will you keep the flame burning? This list should be reviewed at regular intervals (i.e., each anniversary or new year) or whenever either partner feels the need. When we are ready to make a marital commitment, we must take great care in what we promise our spouses. Typically, wedding vows create impossibly high expectations, such as "til death do us part," and if that doesn't work out, we often consider ourselves huge failures before friends, family, and God. In so doing, we create psychological landmines for ourselves. More reasonable vows might be something like, "I choose to take this journey with you and I will fight for our love. I am committed to this journey and will work to stay on it as long as possible." If vows are to be sincerely meaningful, they should also be realistic and reflect the hard work that such a commitment requires.

By setting these standards in place as your compass, it becomes easier to tell when your relationship is off course. Then, you just need the courage to correct your course—together. If you do this and still can't seem to work through your issues, it might become clear that the issue is one of incompatibility not fully explored in the initial stages of the relationship. Or one or both partners took a left turn somewhere. This can make a breakup, if it indeed occurs, much less of a personal rejection and more a difference in philosophy, goals, or priorities. The very act of setting intentions up front can tell you if you are compatible and greatly improve the likelihood of staying together.

Cheating is only one way to ungracefully exit a relationship. Sometimes, people leave without notice. We've probably all heard the story about the parent who "went out for cigarettes" and never came back. That type of betrayal is even more confusing for the people left behind, because they don't know the reason why. Plus, there can be concern. Is the person dead on the side of the road? Or did she really leave? Those left behind tend to foster negative beliefs about themselves as a result of an unexplained exit, as was the case for my friend Meg. This goes back to that compounding trauma I discussed at the beginning.

Sometimes people who break up have the wherewithal to have a conversation with their partners to say they "just can't do this anymore," but they haven't done enough soul-searching to give an explanation. Albeit better than cheating or ghosting, this also can cause some confusion for those left behind, which makes it difficult for them to move on. So, if you're going to have the conversation—and you should, unless you fall into the "exception" category—you're already creating pain for the other party. You might as well find a way to diplomatically let them know why you're leaving.

If you can't verbalize the reason, I highly recommend that you seek personal counseling until you can. This way, you can determine whether the problem is your partner or your own personal baggage. If the latter, saying goodbye to your current partner won't solve the problem, and you will carry that baggage into your next relationship and repeat the process all over again. Your best bet in this situation is to seek personal counseling or talk to a close friend to dig into the source of your dysfunction. If you are able to understand why you behave this way and develop tools to manage it, your partnership may have a chance to thrive.

However, if you are no longer on the same page with your partner and there is no bringing the relationship back, it is important to be honest without being hurtful in communicating your need for an exit. First, assess if your partner will be surprised by this news. If the answer is "yes" or "probably," then you have created your own monster. Surprise is the worst scenario (i.e., compounding trauma). By not airing your complaints along the way, you deny your partner the opportunity to make corrections. They will be justifiably angry at this seemingly sudden change of heart. This is a key moment to pause before proceeding. Instead of pulling the plug, have the conversation about what isn't working for you. It may seem like a pain in the ass, but it allows your partner to make adjustments and/or to see the exit coming.

If the exit still needs to happen, there are some specifics to consider.

First, think about how the other person would want to hear this message. For example, taking someone out to a fancy restaurant to break up with them is just cruel. Your motives may be to avoid a scene, but the lack of consideration you show by doing this may cause one. Second, be equally willing to leave or stay once you deliver the news to the other person. Generally, people want privacy in this situation and may want you to leave immediately while they digest the information so be prepared for that. Or they may want you to stay for hours to talk through what is happening. You should be ready to do that as well.

This period will be difficult for both of you; however, you have already done your own soul-searching. It is now time for you to recognize how your decision affects your partner and empathize with their pain. This will be uncomfortable and the point at which you might want to curse my name and abandon ship. However, if you ride out the discomfort and face your fears, you will be pleasantly surprised at what awaits on the other side. Short-term discomfort is a reasonable price to pay for a lifetime with a clear conscience.

The most important question to ask yourself before sharing this painful news is, *Can I frame the words in a way that allows my partner to hear me?* I promise that if you take the time to put yourself in their shoes, as uncomfortable as that may be, you will be surprised by how well the message can be received. I also promise that if you do not, you will reap what you sow and spend more time and effort working through the aftermath. Remember, the pain you cause is the pain you carry.

I firmly believe the key lesson here is to own our truth and have an honest and compassionate conversation with our partner to let him or her know that our feelings have changed. We do the greatest of services for ourselves and for the one with whom we once fell in love when we alleviate as much of the traditional guilt, unnecessary pain, and betrayal. If there are children involved, it becomes imperative that we do this work to minimize the damage passed on to them. Let's take a look at this most difficult of exit circumstances.

WHAT ABOUT THE KIDS?

One place where grace is sadly missing but desperately needed is in family court services, where custody battles often occur. I have witnessed this system up close with extended family members and it can be traumatic. Couples who once loved one another enough to procreate become opponents captained by lawyers eager to hurl accusations like Molotov cocktails in front of the judge. In the courtroom, folks seem so invested in "winning" that they can no longer see what is best for the children involved. Egos often rage in this environment, which is fundamentally toxic to grace.

For grace to exist, we must have the ability to put ourselves in the shoes of our children, first and foremost. Only then can we feel compassion and see our way to do the right thing. If this feels impossible, I highly recommend reading *The Good Divorce* by Dr. Constance

Ahrons, who pioneered guidance on achieving healthy divorces. The goal is for both parents and children to emerge from the divorce as healthy as they were before it. Her work was the result of a twenty-year study of ninety-eight postdivorce families called "The Binuclear Family Study."

As a divorced mother, I can say that divorce is one of the hardest things I have ever done. For the sake of my children's health and happiness, I required a graceful path. I recall one particular moment in a Target parking lot where I had to explain my ex's new relationship to my then six- and nine-year-olds a few months after our separation. My youngest asked, "Are Daddy and his girlfriend sleeping together?" to which my oldest quickly responded, "No, that would be illegal!" Kids ask the darnedest questions sometimes! I looked to the sky, mentally asking anyone up there who might be listening, "Really? I have to be the one to explain this? You must be joking! How strong do you think I am?"

My kids looked at me with their big, questioning eyes. I took a deep breath and calmly explained what I could about love and the changing nature of relationships. It seemed to satisfy them in the moment, and I quickly changed the subject by saying, "Who's ready to go shopping?"

There are many more stories I could tell that would make you laugh and cry at the cruelty of this path, but I fought my need to be right or validated on more occasions than I wish to share. The result? We now have two young men who love and spend time with their parents both apart and, at times, together. We have come a long way since the divorce. The hard work we did at the beginning—biting our tongues—has paid off tenfold. We now spend holidays together. One summer, the four of us even built a deck in my backyard.

If I ever doubted that my work in this area was meaningful, I received all the confirmation I needed the Christmas Eve I invited my ex and his girlfriend over for the first time. The next day, my oldest son posted a picture on Instagram with the caption, "I can't remember the last time I spent Christmas Eve with my dad. So, I'd say that was the best gift." Ouch. Keeping children from their parents (unless they are dangerous or abusive) is hurtful. No matter how "right" or justified we are, it's just not about us. It's about the kids.

THE BLUEBERRIES

A lovely gentleman named Joe with whom I once had the pleasure of working used to say, "There's a blueberry in there somewhere," using the blueberries in a muffin as a metaphor for getting down to the good stuff. Joe, the chief information officer at the company where I spent most of my career, was an interesting guy who was born in a concentration camp and able to see people's auras. He had a partnership stake in the company but walked away before realizing the big payout to come. He had a beautiful wife and young son at home. Joe died suddenly less than two years after he resigned. I believe he intuited the proximity of his final exit and prioritized his own blueberries just in time—a gorgeous reminder to honor our internal knowing and act accordingly.

Here are some blueberries for those of us who love summaries (be grateful, it could have been a flowchart!).

- Know *why* you want an exit. Do the internal work to understand if and why an exit is necessary. Seek unbiased counseling if needed.
- Wherever you go, there you are. If the problem is you (as a result of trauma, disorders, etc.), swapping out relationships won't solve anything.
- There should be no surprises. Communication is key to staying current with the status of any relationship.
- Plan for predictable exits. Stay out of denial and focus on the now.
- If an exit must occur, communicate your decision in a way that is best for the receiver of the news.
- Recognize and empathize with the other person's pain and then help shepherd the other to find support elsewhere.
- Do your own internal work to find healing and improve yourself as needed for future relationships.

Part II

PROFESSIONAL

Where the needs of the world and your talents cross, there lies your vocation. —Aristotle

For far too many of us, starting a new job is like dating. At first you are curious but somewhat skeptical. Then after several good interviews, your hopes rise and you begin to wonder if this might be "the one." Could this be the place where you will find the success you have been seeking since you entered the workforce?

The interview process is uncannily similar to the courting process in that we dress up, show our "best selves," and tell the other person what we think she wants to hear in order to be considered the best possible match. Sadly, just as with dating, these rituals do not best prepare us for success in terms of long-term compatibility and realistic expectation setting. As a result, the hiring manager might think the applicant is a better fit for the position than he actually is, and the applicant may form expectations of a long-term commitment that is not guaranteed.

Often, companies clearly outline practices for handling nonperforming or policy-breaking employees. Great companies clearly define expectations for job performance and measure it consistently. However, few companies create policies for a reduction in the workforce or layoff of nonexecutive employees. Most simply follow the letter of the law, which may dictate a certain amount of notice if the number of affected employees exceeds a predetermined quantity. Other than that, the most common approach is to get it over with as quickly as possible once the decision has been made.

It doesn't have to be this way. I propose that both companies and employees are better served by setting expectations at the beginning of the work relationship, when both parties are mutually enamored. Although the conversation might be slightly awkward (like asking your new romantic partner for a communicable disease test), the disclosure of a fair separation policy can increase the company's desirability in the applicant's eyes and may even seal the deal. It sends the message that the company is honest and up front about this type of reality. If no such policy exists, the applicant should inquire about company stability and layoff history during the interview process, much like one would ask about past relationships on a third date.

Please note, I am not suggesting that applicants fire off questions about layoffs and company performance during an initial interview. Rather, find more subtle ways to vet the company during courtship. If the company is public, you can research it online, where there is usually a wealth of information about performance and reductions in force via press releases and quarterly reports. If the company is private, you can check online for employee reviews on websites like Glassdoor and Indeed. If you cannot find what you seek, it might make sense to reach out to individuals within the company to get a feel for the true culture and history. For example, you might lunch or meet with a tenured member of the department you wish to join before accepting a job offer. This way you can talk with a potential peer about her experiences without corporate-speak from the human resources department or hiring manager. Ask about how both nonperforming and high-performing employees are treated. Ask about layoffs: Have they occurred? How were employees treated in terms of notice, transfer opportunities, and severance? How is the company's performance? Is there transparency? If so, how are employees informed? Has there been volatility in the past? If so, what caused it?

You get the idea. It's like asking your fiancé's ex about what he was really like after the honeymoon phase (without all of the jealousy and comparisons). By now, you might be thinking, "Jeez, Geri, you sure take the fun out of courtship." Yes—but only a fraction. I would rather take a fraction of the fun out of the courtship process to ensure both parties have the proper expectations than experience a landslide of disappointment later when the stakes are higher. Even if you discover during courtship that the company doesn't have a policy or has a questionable track record, you may still choose to take the job. But do so with the proper expectations. This job may end up being Mr. Right Now, not Mr. Right.

When an ungraceful exit happened to me professionally, I knew it was time to say something. I always tried to treat my employees with respect and worked for companies that allowed me to do so. In turn, I was witness to the amazing strength of the human spirit under very difficult circumstances. The concerns of upper management were the same every time: What about repercussions? Wouldn't it be better to walk laid-off employees out the same day? What if someone sabotaged the business? Won't it bother the retained employees if they have to work with those who they know are leaving?

Just the opposite! No one wants to be treated like a criminal and be ripped from his or her work family without notice. Very few people would be willing to risk their reputation, severance, or freedom by deliberately trying to hurt the company or their coworkers during a moment of frustration. Speaking of coworkers, *no one* feels better when employees simply disappear or take the walk of shame escorted by security and carrying their box of personal items.

One mistake I've seen companies make with regard to setting expectations is to create slogans or mission statements with promises they have no business making. One company for which I worked briefly after an acquisition told its newly acquired employees, "We want to be the last company you ever work for." Eighteen months later, after I had already left, the company laid off everyone at that office. This caused deep bitterness almost a decade later among those involved. It's no different than those unrealistic marriage vows I talked about earlier. Why even go there?

Remember, employees don't need to be lied to in order to stay. Most people need their jobs. Despite the fears of upper management, I have never seen a mass exodus of employees after an announcement or company meeting. It is far better to come in soft with honest communication about what you do and don't know about the company's future. I've seen time and again how much respect and trust honest communication inspires.

Chapter Three

Abandon Ship or Walk the Plank?

Many a false step was made by standing still. —Tim Ferriss[1]

I have seen many people come and go during my more than thirty years in the workforce. No longer does it shock me to see people moving on, and I definitely don't take it personally. But that was not always the case. At the beginning of my management career, I believed that all I needed to be successful was for my team to like me. How do you think that went?

THE FAIL

Early during my career in management, a key employee whom I'll call Kate quit on me out of the blue, giving only two days' notice. I was shocked and betrayed that this individual I had counted on would exit so suddenly without discussing it with me first. I didn't even know she was unhappy! Weren't we part of a family? I really took it personally.

I discussed the situation with my mentor, Beth. She pointed out that perhaps I hadn't kept in touch with Kate's needs, which contributed to my shock that she might want to work elsewhere. She also asked if I had suggested a counteroffer in order to keep Kate. *What an interesting idea.* I had never considered it.

I went back to Kate and admitted my error in not keeping in touch with her needs and working on a career path with her. I asked what caused her to look elsewhere and what it would take for her to stay and be satisfied at our company. She was surprised by my question and apology but became defensive; she had already mentally "left the building." This situation was no different than a lover harboring growing disdain for a partner without communicating anything was amiss and then pulling the plug with little warning or reason. In the end, Kate moved on somewhat ungracefully—and I learned a valuable lesson.

THE BETTER WAY

The key for both manager and employee is to make needs and desires known. With Kate, I should have held regular meetings with her and discussed her level of satisfaction, interests, and desired career path within the organization. By knowing her expectations, I'd be able to identify whether there were compatible opportunities in the organization to meet them. If it became clear that there was not a viable career path for Kate within the organization, she might not be willing to remain long term. Then I could adjust my own expectations accordingly—perhaps investing my development time with another member of the team. In fact, I began this very practice after Kate left—with much success.

However, since it takes two to tango, we must also ask what Kate might have done differently to ensure a better outcome. She could have requested a career path meeting with me to make her needs known and inquire about future opportunities. There is no reason to wait for your boss to bring up this subject with you. Most companies have, at minimum, annual performance reviews, a perfect time for this type of discussion. Additionally, this conversation could have started during the interviewing process, when Kate was considering joining the company, by asking questions like, "How many people have you promoted from your department in the last year?"

It may be uncomfortable to be so direct, but if your goal is to move up in the company, then it must be done. As previously discussed with regard to my marriage, it is always better to identify needs and expectations as early as possible in the relationship to ensure long-term compatibility.

Perhaps something changed for Kate that caused her needs and expectations to change. Perhaps she needed a shorter commute, more money, or different work hours. These are all things that come up in life and sometimes can be negotiated with one's boss. It absolutely doesn't hurt to ask. If you do not have a boss receptive to this type of conversation, you can usually go to the human resources department, where you can request that the discussion be kept confidential.

Okay, let's say you've done all of this and decide the best path is still to leave the company. You're ready to move on, but what is the best way to go about it? Although it may sound fun to tell your boss you're out by posting it on social media, this is not a tactic I recommend. When at all possible, leave those bridges intact because you never know when you might need them.

How and when do you communicate your exit? *First, become very clear about why you are leaving.* Some reasons are easy and logical and meet with little resistance or conflict. Here are some examples:

- I just won the lotto and I really don't need to work anymore.
- I am retiring.
- My spouse has been transferred and we are moving out of state.
- I am staying home to take care of my kids.

In these situations, the goal would be to tell your boss first and give him or her as much notice as possible, like all graceful exits. If your boss hears it through the grapevine first, it will never be well received.

However, what if you simply don't like your job and have found a better one? How honest should or can you be with your boss? In an ideal world, your boss is already aware of your career goals and whether or not there is a desirable path for you in the company. Responsibility for this discussion lies with both parties. If there is not such a path and you choose to move on, it will be no surprise. That conversation is much easier to have. However, if you have not engaged in a career-path discussion with your boss, he or she may be shocked when you announce your planned departure. In this situation, you need to think like a boss and cover your bases. Make your departure as easy as possible by proposing (if you can) how you should be replaced. Who is ready in the organization to fill your shoes? You may need to put your ego aside because everyone really is replaceable. What is your plan for handing off the critical items or projects on which you are working?

If you have answers for these objections, it allows your boss to accept the change more easily. Often, the thoughts running through a boss's mind when an employee gives notice are: What did I do wrong? Who is going to do this person's work? If you can address these two things up front, it will be easier for your boss to digest the news.

Once I was offered a job in a new and emerging industry by an old friend with whom I very much enjoyed working. Because my current company had a questionable future and the terms of the offer were enticing, I knew it was time to make a change. To make the decision more challenging, the timing wasn't great to leave my current job, as I was responsible for a major system conversion planned for that year. I was so conflicted! On one hand, I had a reliable income in an industry that I knew well, working with people I loved. On the other hand, I had an offer in a growing industry that provided a new career path for me. Because I take my responsibilities seriously, I struggled with the idea of abandoning my team, so I asked myself, "What would it take to make my departure work?"

First, I needed to find my replacement. As it turned out, I had a replacement who knew the systems involved and had the conversion management experience needed to fill my shoes at this critical juncture. Because of these extraordinary circumstances, I was able to make the leap and maintain a positive relationship with my former employer after I departed. Although these circumstances may be unique, giving this level of consideration to one's exits doesn't have to be.

If you like your job but are simply leaving for more money, you should always give your boss the opportunity to pay you more to keep you. If you are good at your job, it often costs the company less to give you an increase than it would be to hire someone new. The worst thing that can happen is that your boss says no and you move on anyway. If you approach this conversation respectfully and frame it as your needs versus the company's low pay, you avoid offending your boss and she remains open to negotiation. The conversation could go something like this: "Hey, Susan, got a minute? I wanted to talk to you about my personal situation. I am at a place in my life where I need to bring in a higher income. I really like working here and don't want to leave but I have to put my financial needs first right now, so I have been looking for other jobs. I found one recently and am considering accepting the offer because they are willing to pay me $X per year. Before I accept,

I wanted to ask if there was some way I might be able to stay here and make this amount. What are your thoughts?"

Give it a try. You might be surprised.

A great example of setting expectations for new employees can be found at Zappos. This online shoe retailer, started by the late innovative entrepreneur Tony Hsieh and now owned by Amazon, is known for outstanding customer service. If employees don't feel up to the task after the company communicates expectations during the first week of training, Zappos offers employees a $1,000 bonus to *leave*, in addition to pay for time worked.

This is an outstanding way of setting expectations at the beginning of the relationship and allowing for a graceful exit up front. Both parties win big, because if the employee is not a good fit, they are incentivized to do what is best for both parties. Since a bad hire can cost a company at least 30 percent of the new hire's expected first year earnings, shelling out a smaller "weed-out" bonus up front is just smart business. The company doesn't waste time continuing to train people who are not a good fit and who might jeopardize the company's reputation.

Inspired by Zappos, Amazon began a similar program for current employees. Once a year, they are given a "pay to quit" letter that encourages them to think about whether they want to continue employment with Amazon. Based on their tenure, they could receive between $2,000 and $5,000 to leave their job. Talk about making it easy to gracefully exit! This is a beautiful way of checking in with each employee to ask, "Are you still enjoying this relationship? Or is it time to move on?" Brilliant!

PREVENTION

As with all relationships, frequent and honest communication is key in the workplace. Before you leave a position, become clear about why you are leaving and then consider whether there are options to stay before making the leap. If it is time to go, always be as kind and considerate as you can so that you remain in good standing. The grass is not always greener, and you never know when you might need a great reference or another job.

As a manager, keep good employees longer by getting to know them, their hopes and dreams, and what is going on in their lives. This will help you to develop informed expectations for your entire team and reduce the shock if an employee chooses to leave. And although having an employee choose to leave is difficult, *asking* an employee to leave is even harder on everyone involved. Let's go there.

GETTING FIRED: YOU'RE *OUT*!

Getting fired can be extremely traumatic if you don't see it coming, yet somewhat graceful if good management practices are in place. I have witnessed both, and it can be ugly when it goes bad. Unlike layoffs, being fired for nonperformance sends a clear message to the employee that he or she is not good enough in the position. If the employee understood what was expected, had the required training, and was given course-correcting feedback the moment he or she began to drift, then the firing should not be a surprise. However, when those key elements are missing, terminated employees can feel set up and even betrayed—not so graceful, right?

Let's look at the differences. I have heard dozens of stories of nonperforming employees either not being terminated because no performance management practices were in place or experiencing spectacularly ungraceful exits that resulted in wrongful termination claims. This is a mess you surely want to avoid. It is up to management to ensure this does not happen. The key here is clarity.

THE FAIL

Let's talk about Michelle, whom I once managed. She was the life of the party—or so it seemed—funny, fun, kept work entertaining, and well-liked by all. She was also a little intimidating and quick to anger when things weren't going her way (definitely a Dr. Jekyll/Mr. Hyde type). As a new supervisor, I was unsure how to rein her in and had no guidance on setting performance expectations. When I began to receive complaints from coworkers and customers about either of her extremes (too chatty or too gruff), I had little structure to fall back on.

Michelle and I had several anecdotal discussions about "the complaints," which caused greater tension in the department and no improvement in performance. At some point, tired of the complaints, I actually tried to fire her but was so vague and out of my depth in terms of concrete logic and reason that we ultimately agreed to "do better next time." I was shocked when she challenged my suggestion that she find employment elsewhere. I can distinctly recall leaving that meeting feeling that I failed but confused about why. I was the boss, I wanted to fire her . . . so what was the problem?

Looking back, I can understand why Michelle could not accept her own termination. There were no clear expectations and, as such, she could see no justifiable reason for being terminated. What a mess!

THE BETTER WAY

All employees need to use the same scorecard with regard to performance to know if they are winning or losing. Setting clear performance standards, as well as a method to measure actual performance against that standard, is the key. This requires some set up and a bit of reworking from time to time, but the payoff in terms of performance and culture is undeniable. Some employers might say, "Why bother? All of my employees are hired 'at will,' so I can fire anyone, anytime."

I respectfully disagree. At-will employment protects employers and evens the playing field between employer and employee in that both parties can initiate a termination of the relationship at any time. This makes sense but does not create a high-performing culture and smooth terminations if needed. You get what you give in all relationships, and a company can't expect loyalty or notice if it isn't willing to give it. By creating a culture in which both employer and employee play by the same set of rules, there is much less drama for both, and performance tends to improve.

Let's get back to Michelle and assume we had a performance scorecard in place. If so, I would meet with Michelle on a regular basis to review her performance and would address the first issue when it arose. In that meeting, I would try to understand what prevented her from performing to the set standard and then remove any valid roadblocks outside her control. If there were none, we would then discuss ways within her control for her to improve.

By doing this, I could get Michelle to buy in to the improvement process, as well as eliminate external causes (or excuses). This first meeting is collaborative and all about solving the problem. Because I have the scorecard, I do not need to be confrontational. I simply discuss what the data tells us (as I have been doing at all of our meetings before the issue arose). This allows Michelle to depersonalize the meeting, since we are looking at one blip on the radar of her performance. Also, because I am collaborative with her, she has the space to suggest ways that she can improve. Without the scorecard, the meeting could be confrontational and feel like a personal attack.

If Michelle has not improved by our next performance checkup, I would clarify that a lack of improvement could result in additional discipline, up to and including termination—albeit not something I want to see happen. I would then ask Michelle her plan for getting back on track. My goal is to make the consequences clear and to place full responsibility for improvement on her shoulders while still offering support.

At the next performance checkup, which would happen at a brief but reasonable interval from our last meeting, we would review the scorecard again. If there was improvement, we would celebrate that, and I would ask Michelle what she did differently to achieve a better result. I would make note of that for future reinforcement, and she would have further proof to the idea that she is in charge of her own performance. If Michelle did not improve, this would be the meeting to either terminate her or place her on probation, with the promise that the next violation (within a reasonable time period) would result in immediate termination.

Determining the number of violations before termination varies depending upon the severity of the violation. For example, if the employee is caught stealing and the employee manual clearly states this is a fireable offense, then you might skip this whole process and terminate immediately. If an employee missed hitting a productivity number one day last week, then it might not make sense to fire someone who has shown general improvement otherwise. You get the idea. With a fourth violation, I would then start the company's termination protocol and my next meeting with Michelle would be our last.

With this process in place, I can be confident that I have done everything I can for Michelle and my conscience is clear.

Coworkers often realize when a peer is not performing. When termination finally occurs after the process described above, they generally come to the same conclusion. It's no fun, but it's the right thing to do. I have seen many terminations with and without such a process in place. Every manager who ever worked for me would agree that managing employees is 100 percent better when you have scorecards. More often than not, managing with performance standards creates a turnaround for the struggling employee and an exit is avoided. When performance can't be improved, scorecards and periodic performance meetings keep the conversation and relationship between the manager and employee objective and fact- and solution-based. If an exit must happen, employees are not surprised and tend to take responsibility for it, which allows for a more graceful experience.

PREVENTION

What about Michelle? What is her role in this? At the first sign of her manager's discontent with her performance, she might have requested a meeting to review expectations. At that time, it would have been a good idea for Michelle to request any process documentation she might need to ensure clarity. She could also request additional training or accommodations. If at any point, despite her best efforts, she realized she wasn't up to the performance level the position required, she could ask about relocating to a better fitting job within the company. If nothing was available in-house, she could begin looking for a new position immediately outside the company while negotiating her exit date. In some cases, the manager might be amenable to this while looking for her replacement to avoid as many gaps in productivity as possible.

If you have been fired and are struggling to accept it, there is an opportunity here for you to become a "better loser." The first step is to make sure you understand why you were fired. If you don't have this information, go back to your employer and get it. Next, examine your role in your termination. Where could you have tried harder or made changes? This part is not easy but valuable for future endeavors.

Once you are clear on your part, do the work required to improve your skill set, attitude, or work ethic. There are great books, webinars, and podcasts covering all of this. And never underestimate the power of a good therapist. Once your work on yourself is underway, move on from thinking about your old job. Bless and release! Make the old job a lesson from which you learned and for which you can now be grateful.

The importance of being a good loser is tied to your future happiness. Many people become stuck in a particularly difficult loss and are unable to move forward. No matter how devastated you might be because it didn't work out, the sun will continue to rise and set. The longer it takes for us to move forward, the more life will pass us by.

Chapter Four

Culling the Herd

It is not the strongest of the species that survives, not the most intelligent that survives. It is the one that is the most adaptable to change.
—Charles Darwin

Layoffs are one of the unfortunate risks of running a business. More than twenty-one million US workers were laid off or fired in 2019, according to the Bureau of Labor Statistics.[1] Then, when the COVID-19 pandemic hit in spring 2020, another twenty million jobs vanished as workplaces shut their doors. Rare is the company that does not have to lay off employees at one time or another—although they do exist (check out Nugget Market, Aflac, and NuStar Energy). Tough economic periods, automation, and acquisitions are just a few of the reasons that often result in employees being laid off to ensure company success or viability. Because layoffs are a common occurrence in business culture, it is surprising to me that more companies do not handle them gracefully.

The impact of layoffs can be traumatic to everyone involved and cause residual effects in the organization. A friend of mine who is an extremely competent and caring human once had to lay off a member of his team. He was so gutted by the experience that he vowed never to hold a management position again and changed his career path as a result. Years later he still carries incredible remorse and worries that he ruined that person's life. Layoffs are not child's play and they should be handled accordingly.

The first time I was required to lay off a large group of people, I felt highly intimidated. The company I worked for had recently acquired a company with multiple offices across the country. Our plan was to consolidate redundant departments, and the employees in the remote offices needed to be notified of this transition simultaneously. As a director, I was required to notify employees I barely knew in the Amarillo, Texas, office, with the assistance of our chief financial officer.

To prepare for this announcement, my company provided training from an outside consultant on how to do it "right." It was a supportive gesture from the executive team, and definitely the right thing to do. The training, however, focused on what to say and how to say it quickly to avoid any ugliness from the audience. The plan was for counselors, who were waiting in the break room, to help employees with their emotions. My job was to get the news out quickly and to hand the employees off to the counselors. I practiced my speech multiple times, traveled to the office, and barely slept the night before the big day.

When we pulled up to the office in the morning, a camera crew from the local news station was set up out front. Apparently, a local employee had tipped them off that "suits" were coming from corporate, and the reporters were sniffing around for a story. I walked into the building without incident but noticed a small sign stenciled on the outside of the building: "Please check concealed weapons with the receptionist."

Gulp. What did I sign up for?

I proceeded to where the staff was assembled, climbed onto the riser set up for me, and looked out on the eighty-plus faces in front of me reflecting concern, fear, doubt, and mistrust. Up until this point, my concerns had been all about me: Why did I have to do this? How scary would it be? Would someone freak out and try to hurt me? When I looked at those nervous faces, I realized it was not about me at all. My discomfort would last only a few moments, but theirs would last so much longer. I delivered my assigned message with as much compassion as possible.

When I was done, someone in the audience raised a hand. According to our consultant, questions weren't on the menu. However, I took it because I could not deny this person information that might help. I answered that question—and then another raised a hand. And then another and another. I stood there answering questions for forty-five minutes, well past the time frame my trainers recommended. The bare minimum I could do was to answer their questions.

I just couldn't walk away from these people. Yes, they would continue working until their work transitioned to corporate, a process of about four weeks. Yes, they would get severance packages based on their years of service. Yes, we would accept their job applications in our corporate office. Yes, I would stay at this office with them during the transition.

Finally, a petite elderly woman raised her hand. When I acknowledged her, she said, "I just want to thank you for being honest with us. My entire retirement savings were invested in this company, which is now worth nothing, and I have only been lied to by [the previous owner]. You have given me more answers in the last hour than I have been able to get in the last year, so thank you."

At this point, I knew I had to wrap up the meeting or I would start crying. I thanked everyone and climbed down from the risers, fighting back tears.

I am grateful that I followed my instincts to stay with the employees as long as they needed. I am grateful that the company allowed me to offer generous packages to the affected employees, which included resume writing services, four weeks of notice, job placement services, and severance. These "perks" allowed me to work side by side with these employees for the next month as they completed their work without incident. The majority of them found their next jobs during that month, and the rest were well on their way. Consequently, their last days were far less traumatic—a little sad, but no one yelled, threatened . . . or pulled any guns.

THE FAIL

Earlier in my career, I worked in the production department at the same company's corporate office in San Diego. Through another acquisition, we picked up a second production department in New York. In an effort to reduce redundancy, the decision was made to close that department and consolidate the work into the corporate office.

Typically, we would have sent a manager to New York to oversee the closure of that facility, as I did in Amarillo. However, there was no one available to handle that type of long-term assignment, and no one in the local office could be counted on, either. These circumstances led to the decision to announce and conduct the layoffs on the same day. To accomplish this, we needed to send a trusted crew to the New York facility to transition the work after terminating the local employees. The planning and preparation for this effort included securing the transition team (the T-Team—we even had a logo) and holding secret planning meetings to review schedules, systems, and roles. We all understood that the transition team would work long hours for several weeks to complete the assignment.

I can honestly say that the planning phase was actually fun. That is, until we had to talk on the phone to someone from the New York office who had no idea what was about to happen. What I personally experienced was extreme guilt, as did most of the folks who knew the axe was about to fall on our friends across the country with whom we spoke on a regular basis. Asking people to keep that type of secret is similar to asking them not to blink—it's painful.

On announcement day, the affected employees in New York were called to an off-site meeting at a local hotel. Apparently, the transition team missed one small detail: the early morning shift arrived at the office a few hours before the meeting, only to find the locks being changed on the office doors. Still, they did not give it a huge amount of thought. They departed on schedule to the off-site meeting like trusting little lambs. It wasn't until they arrived at the hotel and noticed no donuts or coffee, something they had come to expect, that they knew something was off. One employee told me that was the exact moment she knew something was very wrong. Isn't it strange that the thing that gave it away was something so small—no donuts?

As employees were notified that their facility would be closed and work moved to corporate, they experienced complete shock. One employee's recollection was that some "lady that she had never met before" stood up in front of everyone and just said, "We are shutting this facility down." People that they considered "their friends at corporate" became the "suits from corporate" letting them go. Adding insult to injury, employees were allowed to return to the office that day but only under the close supervision of security guards while they cleaned out their desks. In just a few hours, they had gone from being trusted employees who worked diligently to produce the company's products, to suspected criminals who needed to be watched every minute. This is a classic example of management demonizing their victims to make such a decision easier on them. It's like when one spouse is cheating and feels guilty, so she picks arguments with the other spouse to justify her actions.

After the New York employees left the building, many went to a local watering hole to deal with the blow they had received. There was much commiserating and company bashing—and a plan to call in to a local radio station the following Friday to vent during a segment called "Take This Job and Shove It." Nothing fuels anger and a desire for revenge quite like betrayal.

Later in the week, the affected employees had to return to the office to meet with a human resources manager to receive their severance packages. When one employee, Cindy, met with the manager, she was not given a severance package. Instead, she was offered a different job, as the company needed a small team to handle support functions for the local sales team. Because she needed the money, Cindy accepted the position. What she didn't anticipate were the repercussions of that decision on her personal life. Because she chose to remain with the company, Cindy lost her closest friend and former coworker who was to be the maid of honor in her upcoming wedding. Her friend felt betrayed and informed Cindy that she would no longer be in contact because Cindy had decided to stay with the company that laid her off. Ouch. This clearly demonstrates that management must look at employees not only as coworkers, but also as friends and even families. Keeping this in mind when making and communicating layoff decisions might make room for a little more grace.

Part of the psychological impact of being laid off without notice is exclusion. You were a part of something—and suddenly you are not any longer. You spent your day with people trying to build something—and suddenly you are cut off. It is similar to a death in terms of your day-to-day interactions, the people you talk to, and the things that you do. To be excluded from that and to know that it is continuing without you can be traumatic. It is disturbing and odd and takes time to adjust to the point that you can feel good about it.

It is also unnecessary. If the employees had notice, they could put a bow on it, say goodbye, and so forth. Because of how it was handled, it takes longer to process and get past it.

THE BETTER WAY

A gentler approach would be to provide as much notice as possible. A great example of this occurred a few years later in my career when we decided to consolidate another business function from the field offices to the corporate office to increase efficiency. At the time, we had six departments doing the same job—five in remote offices around the country and one at the corporate office. Because daily work volume fluctuated at each office, especially directly before and after a commission cutoff, the employees in the remote locations worked massive amounts of overtime to make the cutoff and then had little work the following week. To accommodate this, we tended to be overstaffed in these functions. By consolidating the work at corporate, we could staff more appropriately while utilizing resources from other departments to handle spikes in volume.

Although the reasons for moving work to our corporate office were similar, in this scenario we were able to take a more graceful route. We used a notification and attrition approach by giving the affected employees a twelve-month notice. We also shared the logic for the consolidation, and although the remote employees didn't like how it affected them personally, they could understand the reason for it and how it helped the business. All employees were offered jobs at the corporate office if they were interested in moving (only one of the thirty employees took this option) or positions in our sales departments in their remote offices. We allowed each remote department to utilize slow periods of work to build resumes and look for work elsewhere. This approach allowed them to find other jobs during the next year, which gave them the luxury of finding a good fit for their needs rather than taking the first job they could find.

Since the notification was so long, we did not feel it necessary to give large severance packages to the affected employees. With this scenario, most business owners and managers would be concerned that the notified employees would sabotage the company or would leave at the same time. This was not a concern, because we had built a strong culture with good leaders in each office. Additionally, there were minimal issues with reductions in productivity, quality, or attitudes. These leaders were loyal to both the company and their staff. As such, they managed the situation to a successful end. Each employee found another job by the end of that year except for one who chose to retire. It was highly successful for both the company and the affected employees, all of whom were treated with respect. Employees were allowed to complete their work, leave on a somewhat positive note, and, most importantly, say goodbye to their friends and coworkers.

Were there difficult moments? Absolutely! It was the corporate department manager's responsibility to staff up as employees in the field transitioned to other jobs. She was required to work closely with her counterparts in the field offices that were being downsized. Immediately after the announcement, conversations became awkward but improved after talking it over. Additionally, morale dipped slightly every time a remote employee found a new job and left. Imagine being happy for your friend and coworker, sad he is leaving, and simultaneously stressed that you still haven't found a job. Quite a rollercoaster.

The managers in the field handled this amazingly well by taking the remaining team to lunch, planning fun events, and using humor on a daily basis. In turn, the managers turned to me and to each other to vent, share concerns, and brainstorm solutions to problems as they arose. The system worked incredibly well. Unlike most layoffs, each departure lacked the anger, shame, and resentment toward the company that one might typically expect. Several employees were later rehired by the company in different roles.

The key lesson from this do-over is that employees will rise to your expectations if you let them. They will also stoop low if you expect the worst from them. In this situation, I was certain the remote teams would rise based on the culture and trust we had built and the strong leadership in place in each of the offices. Obviously, a year's notice is not workable in all scenarios, but the concept can be adapted to almost any situation. If you cannot give a long notice, do what you can to offer a generous severance package. If that's not possible either, then give what you can and offer other options: part-time work, work in other departments, job placement services, access to an employee assistance program. There are laws for layoffs that must be followed with regard to notice, so make sure you are on proper legal footing before you do anything. See www .dol.gov/compliance/laws/comp-warn.htm for more information.

According to Lisa Cullen in a 2007 *Time* magazine article:

> Layoffs have a staggering effect not just on the laid off but on everybody in the workplace. It affects our performance . . . our families . . . it knocks

about our emotional equilibrium, hobbles our confidence, widens our chasm of self doubt.[2]

It seems to be the norm that upper management so often underestimates the attachment front-line workers feel for their jobs. They seem to forget that our jobs are an important part of our identities and how we spend the majority of our waking hours. We tend to assume that if we work hard enough, our job will be secure, perhaps because we want to believe that life is fair or because we have no idea the company may be struggling. Transparency goes a long way toward keeping expectations realistic.

Here are a few important things to remember if you are ever placed in the position of laying off an employee—or if you're trying to improve the way you do it:

- Remember, it's not about you.
- Ask yourself how you would want to be treated.
- Banish your own defensiveness and show up with empathy and love.
- Give each employee a clear reason why this is happening.
- Apologize—your company is at fault in a layoff—not the employee.
- Give employees notice.
- Give employees the best severance package you can.

If you need further inspiration to take the graceful exit path at your company, watch or rewatch the critically acclaimed movie *Up in the Air*. In it, George Clooney plays human resource transition specialist Ryan Bingham. Various companies hire Ryan's firm to do the dirty work of layoffs for them—the ultimate insult. The opening scene is a montage of employee reactions to the bad news, which are just as bad as you would expect. Here are a couple of my favorite employee reactions:

- "On a stress level, I've heard that losing your job is like a death in the family, but personally, I feel more like the people I worked with were my family and I died."
- "I think the anger comes from the fact that I just wasn't needed anymore."

Ryan is training a rookie throughout the movie, and this is how he describes his job:

- "Now just remember . . . don't tell them how hard this is for you. Today's one of the worst days they're ever going to have in their life. How we feel doesn't compare."
- "We are here to make limbo tolerable—to ferry wounded souls across the river of dread until the point where hope is dimly visible . . . and then stock the boat, shove them in the water, and make them swim. This is what we do. . . . We take people at their most fragile and set them adrift."
- "And that's because I don't work here. I work for another company that lends me out to pussies like Steve's boss who don't have the balls to sack their own employees, and in some cases, for good reason, because people do crazy shit when they get fired."

Speaking of the "crazy shit" that people do when they get fired or laid off, such concerns are understandable but not statistically probable. In 2020, there were 392 workplace fatalities caused by assault, according to the National Safety Council.[3] These deaths include nonworker-on-worker assaults, the most common being customer assaults on taxi drivers and healthcare workers. During this period, forty-one million workers were laid off or fired in the United States according to the US Bureau of Labor Statistics.[4] Thus, the risk of an extreme result is less than .00001 percent. That said, the best insurance against violent reactions is to foster a culture of respect and loyalty *before* the need for layoffs occurs. Additionally, training management to spot warning signs of mental health issues is an important step. Treating employees with respect and giving them notice along with some severance goes a long way toward ensuring that they behave constructively until their last day.

PREVENTION

As a business owner or manager, it is your duty to hire responsibly. Often leaders get ahead of themselves or fall in love with a candidate, even though the demand for his services has not fully developed. I was taught to view each new hire as a commitment—I would provide a job and in turn she would work hard for me. Taking such a commitment seriously forced me to continuously look for opportunities to maximize efficiency. Additionally, every time a position was vacated, we seriously questioned whether that position needed to be filled. The entire department worked through this exercise, which promoted inclusion and problem solving within the team. Department members often surprised me by stepping up to do more and coming up with new ideas to avoid adding head count, which positively impacted the bottom line.

In addition to staffing conservatively, it is important that the top brass view layoffs as a last resort. Always consider creative options before choosing to let people go. One option I have used to cut costs without reducing head count is to institute a holiday furlough program, in which employees are required to take off the last two weeks of the calendar year whether or not they have vacation time. Because this was a slow period for the business, it allowed the company to save some money and get vacation accruals off the books. It also meant that more employees were available during other periods of the year when their attendance was critical. Finally, consistent performance management is critical to prevent layoffs. Daily and weekly productivity and accuracy standards are the key to ensuring that each team is working toward its maximum capacity. Remember, you are responsible for every person you hire.

PARTIAL DEPARTMENT LAYOFFS: CANADIAN *IDOL*

Another wrinkle to the subject of department layoffs or workforce reductions is partial layoffs. This happens when the manager needs to reduce the total head count of the department by a certain number of employees. This is especially difficult on managers, who are put in the position of playing God with their staff's lives. Not fun. Some companies determine the layoff group based on seniority (hire date), but this is not always the best way to go. You may be left with lower performing, more expensive employees while newer, more productive or accurate talent leaves.

So, what is a manager to do? First, let's talk about what *not* to do.

THE FAIL

A horrifying account of a layoff was shared with me by a Canadian coworker. This story serves as a classic example of what *not* to do, the reason for which will soon become obvious. Apparently, the company decided on slash-and-burn layoffs, in which folks were given no notice and asked to leave the same day. This method is especially cruel because it doesn't allow employees time: (1) to mentally process the news (including understanding the whys); (2) to complete work in progress (important to most employees); and (3) to say goodbye to coworkers (with whom they have spent more time than most of their friends and family).

These are three critical elements to any exit, which enable closure and allow those affected to move on. A great HBO show, *The Leftovers*, based on the 2011 novel by Tom Perrotta, demonstrates this beautifully. It shows the impact on the people left behind when loved ones suddenly disappear with no notice or explanation. The opening scene shows a mother loading her car with groceries while her baby cries from the car seat in the backseat. She turns away from the baby to grab the next bag of groceries from the cart when the baby suddenly stops crying. When the mom turns around, the baby has vanished. Cars can be heard crashing in the distance. Screams follow. The psychological impact is massive. Those left behind never understand why; they have to move on without getting a chance to say goodbye. It is a disturbing premise for a show, but we see and experience similar events in bad exits all the time.

I digress. When you are laying off a portion of your workforce, it is always tough to figure out how to tell both the employees who are leaving and those who are staying. With slash-and-burn layoffs, that becomes particularly difficult. According to my Canadian friend, his company decided to cut down a department by separating employees into two different meeting rooms (sounds like *American Idol*), giving one group the good news and one the bad news. Although this is horrifying enough for a variety of reasons, the fatal flaw came when the employees were herded into rooms next to each other—rooms with fabric-covered, semi-permanent, not-at-all-soundproof walls.

Imagine being in the "good news" room. After hearing the news, the initial flood of relief washes over you. Then you begin to realize who is *not* in the room. It dawns on you that some of your coworkers and friends are now deep in shock; you can hear them crying or yelling right next door. You get the picture. When you leave the meeting, your fears are confirmed as you collide with coworkers from the "other room." Talk about survivor's guilt.

On the other hand, if you are in the "bad news" room, insult has been added to injury when your friends and coworkers witness your stunned exit. You feel, for the first time, the overwhelming separateness of your realities. This is just shameful and unnecessarily traumatic.

This makes me angry because it is so easy to avoid. The irony is that the company handled the layoffs this way to make it as quick and painless (for the company) as possible, but I guarantee you that people will speak badly about that company for the rest of their lives. My friend told me this story several years after the layoff, when he had moved on to something much better. Nonetheless, he couldn't say enough bad things about his former employer.

THE BETTER WAY

What's the alternative to this type of nightmare layoff? I'd like to offer a great example I was fortunate enough to experience. A company for which I worked needed to reduce the size of one of my departments by a third due to declining demand in the industry (telephone directories— need I say more?). The manager and I agreed that the fairest approach was to lay off the lowest performers in terms of productivity, accuracy, and dependability. Additionally, we were able to give all employees notice, both of the impending layoffs and of the method we would use for determining who stayed and who left. This gave all employees in the department time (about two months) to make sure that they were performing at their best, consistently, before the bottom third was selected.

This may seem like a lot of work. Wouldn't it be easier to just pick the bottom third and walk them out the door on day one? As shown by the Canadian *Idol* anecdote, the problem with that approach is that not only do you eliminate a key ingredient for a graceful exit (no surprises), but you also shake the confidence of the remaining two-thirds of the employees still working for the company. It would be natural for the "leftovers" to think "if they treat my coworkers this way, why wouldn't they also treat me this way in the future?" This might severely damage the culture well after their coworkers have gone. Additionally, by giving the department notice of what is coming, employees who were planning to leave in the near future could step forward to resign, thereby saving another's job.

The bottom line: people want to be told the truth. Lying is insulting. People generally understand that bad things can happen. Plans change and life disappoints. Therefore, if a business struggles, it would not be unreasonable to expect a layoff. But when management lies to cover up "trouble," the layoff is compounded by betrayal. Betrayal is what causes folks to go postal.

A quick search on LinkedIn or Google yields several articles that confirm this process. In "How to Conduct a Layoff" on www.nolo.com, author Bethany Laurence states, "The lesson to be learned from these fiascoes is clear: Be respectful when you lay workers off. . . . Involve the top brass. Layoffs are a major event and should be handled by top company executives."[5]

In the human resources community, the general consensus is to give as much notice as possible. Tell the affected employees individually what is happening. Explain why it is happening. Express compassion and gratitude for the contributions the affected employees have made and then let them know what will happen next in terms of benefits, saying goodbye to their peers, severance, their personal belongings, and so forth. It's important to remember that some employees will be in shock and therefore unable to absorb all the information provided. Give them clear written instructions to take home and offer an option for follow-up conversations if needed.

INDIVIDUAL LAYOFFS: IT'S NOT ME, IT'S YOU

Individual layoffs are less frequent than multiperson layoffs, but they do happen when a company needs to restructure or reduce head count to improve efficiency or respond to slow or stagnant growth. Also, they tend to apply to management positions or individuals who work independently. Regardless, the same rules apply in terms of the right and wrong approaches. Let's look at an example near and dear to my heart.

THE FAIL

Remember when I told you about being laid off by a dear friend at the beginning of this book? Here's the whole story. I got a great job offer in an emerging technology market when my old friend, Mike, contacted me. We had a work history of more than twenty-five years between two companies. Mike begged me to leave my position as chief operating officer at a publishing firm to work with him once again. He recently had joined the board of a new company and needed my assistance because he intended to ramp up sales aggressively, as he had done at his two previous companies. He needed me to prepare the operations organization to accommodate that growth. After declining several times, he made an offer I couldn't refuse, and I made the leap.

Fast forward nine months. The projected sales increase never materialized, and the company was under great pressure to perform. My department was performing well, and we had a model that could handle growth when it eventually came, but without an increase in sales, there really was no point. On a Friday afternoon, my friend and boss called to let me know that the board met and "we had to make some cuts." As I already described, this was not a new concept for me, and my response was, "Okay, what do you need me to do?"

Mike then said, "Actually, Geri, it's you. We have to let you go."

I was immediately locked out of my company e-mail and business platforms.

Well, you could have knocked me over with a feather—not because it didn't make business sense, but because each of us believes (to varying degrees) it will never happen to us—until it does. Also, Mike had begged me to come, and the reason the business could no longer afford me was because he was not successful in generating sales. But most of all, he chose to tell me over the phone, with no warning, effective immediately. As a highly experienced executive with a long and positive history of working with Mike, it was ludicrous to be treated this way. Yet it also reminded me that it doesn't matter what your title is. Being treated this way is offensive at any level.

It felt awful to be cut off from my team, with whom I had grown close. I wanted to explain and reassure them that they could handle this transition. I wanted to hand off the work in progress to avoid confusion or disruption. I wanted to wrap up deals with outside vendors to ensure a smooth transition. Yet I was unable to do any of this because I was cut off immediately. All of this from a friend I had known for more than twenty-five years. It made zero sense to me and I felt furious, shocked, and betrayed.

In the days that followed, I suffered through a grieving process, as you might with a death in the family. I also learned more details that added insult to injury. My "friend" had actually traveled to my city to tell me in person but backed out at the last minute. He couldn't bear to have the conversation face to face, so he left town and called me instead. I also realized that my employment contract required thirty days' notice, which I clearly didn't receive, so at least I picked up an additional month of severance. The fact that no one thought to look at the agreement before pulling the trigger speaks to how quickly they wanted to get it over with—like ripping off a damn Band-Aid.

The way in which this particular layoff was handled caused both my friend and me much unnecessary anguish. Additionally, my staff was shaken by my sudden departure because they saw me as a trusted member of the executive team. When I suddenly was gone without notice, it shook their faith in the company. If I could be treated this way, they rightfully reasoned, it would be foolish to think they would be treated any better.

THE BETTER WAY

For this do-over, I want to walk through the same example (because it's a good one and also extremely cathartic). After the board meeting where it was decided to cut costs, one option could have been for the executive team to come together to brainstorm how this might happen. I have experienced this in other positions, and it fosters bonding since each team member contributes to the overall need. One option might have been to ask each of the executives to chip in part of their salary to help share the burden and weather the storm. If nothing else, this exercise serves two purposes: exposing opportunities to cut costs and giving warning to the team that there is a dire need for such measures. If, after such a meeting, it becomes apparent that the identified cuts are not enough, then it is time to go to the next level—staff reductions.

In this do-over, it likely would still make sense to phase out my position, since the expected growth did not happen. The graceful way to handle this would have been for Mike to set up a face-to-face meeting and say something like, "As you know, we are not close to meeting our cost-cutting goal after our meeting. We have looked at every position and because I was not able to build sales as promised, the company cannot support someone of your caliber at this time. I realize that I brought you here, and I am so sorry that I wasn't able to make it work. You have a thirty-day-notice clause in your contract that you can exercise, or you can choose to shorten that if you can hand your work off sooner. What do you need from me?"

In his blog "How to Handle a Layoff" for *Harvard Business Review*, Steve Robbins has similar suggestions:

> Never delegate pain. . . . The person's manager should deliver the message. Deliver the message personally, respectfully—and listen. . . . People have different reactions—some need to vent, some need time to think, and some need facts and explanations.[6]

After a conversation like this, I would have been able to hand off work in progress and prep my team for the transition. I could have said goodbye to my friends and coworkers and left on a positive note. My friend could have felt much better about the hard decision he made by necessity. We could have talked during the transition process and worked out the awkward emotional stuff that arises in a situation like this. If my friend had just a few minutes of courage to look me in the eye, sit with me in my shock, and give me the benefit of the doubt that I would act in both the company's and my own best interests, we could have taken positive action.

Some folks might argue that allowing such an exit exposes the company to risk, but I argue that the opposite does so. Treating people poorly is what causes extreme and violent reactions. Showing respect calls upon their better nature. I have seen it hundreds of times firsthand. Additionally, if the person to be laid off was known as a loose cannon before any such announcement, he or she could and should be terminated for poor performance instead of being laid off. This sends a more accurate and reasonable message to the rest of the organization. Remember, how you treat each employee tells the rest of the team what they can expect from you. If you want to build a cohesive culture where folks go that extra mile, you need to be trustworthy in both your words and deeds.

PREVENTION

The formula for prevention is the same here as with other layoffs: don't hire until you are sure you can support the position. On the flip side, don't take a job until you are sure the company can support your position for the foreseeable future. Always look for efficiencies to keep your team as lean as reasonable while still providing excellent service/output.

Create a culture of continuous improvement and include employees at all levels in imagining that improvement. Encourage employees that are so inclined to work themselves out of their current job and to aim for a better one. Some employees withhold good ideas that might result in less work for them because they are not confident that the company will retain them once such improvements are in place. However, if the company culture encourages and rewards such innovations, employees are more likely to bring these ideas to management. Finally, be transparent about the overall health of the company so that everyone has a realistic picture.

Once again this is backed up by Stever Robbins in the aforementioned blog:

> Communicate widely and often—managers often think they shouldn't let employees know when things are going poorly. They don't want their workers to become discouraged. But people aren't stupid; they know when things aren't going well. . . . If layoffs become necessary, people won't be shocked if they have been able to see them coming.[7]

By letting your team in on major challenges, you make room for creative solutions you might not have considered. A great example of this occurred in 2020 at Gravity Payments, founded by Dan Price and made famous by his $70,000 minimum wage implemented in 2015. When the pandemic hit small and medium businesses in March 2020, Gravity saw a 55 percent drop in revenue. Price's options seemed daunting—cut staff by 20 percent or run out of cash in five months. Instead of jumping to layoffs, Price opted for transparency and shared the details of the challenge at a company-wide meeting.

This is where the magic happened. Almost all of the employees volunteered to cut their pay to keep the company afloat, some offering 100 percent of their salary for the short term. The end result? The employee

wage cuts bought the company time and actually resulted in higher performance, which allowed Gravity to restore employee salaries within
four months and pay back the money its employees sacrificed during
that time. This is such an amazing and inspiring example of the power
of collective problem solving.[8]

Another thing to remember is that layoffs can be just as hard, if not
harder, on the manager conducting them. Similar to my conversation
with my ex-husband when he shared the guilt he carried for his actions,
I had a conversation with Mike. We had gone many years without
speaking, separated both by distance and a bit of awkwardness. One
day, he reached out after learning my sons were in Houston during
Hurricane Harvey. From there, we kept in touch occasionally, but never
spoke about how our working relationship ended.

While I was working on this book, I knew it was time to face him. I
was going to be traveling near his home and asked if I could visit. He
welcomed me with open arms and a lovely meal with him and his wife.
We caught up on events over the many years that had passed. After
dinner, I asked him if he ever thought about how he handled my exit.
"Aw, Ger, I cried about it just the other day," he replied (again with
surprising speed).

Mike's a big softy, to be honest, and it felt great for him to finally
talk about how much my layoff had pained him. It was obvious that he
carried the weight of that exit much harder and longer than I did. Like
I said, the pain you cause is the pain you carry.

THE BLUEBERRIES

Just as we did at the end of Part I, we will capture the important stuff
at the end of each part and call them "blueberries." An homage to my
friend Joe who used to say, "there's a blueberry in there somewhere,"
using the blueberries in a muffin as a metaphor for getting down to the
good stuff.

- Get to know your staff's hopes and dreams to avoid surprise exits.
- Create and maintain clear performance expectations so everyone fol-
  lows the same set of rules.

- Problem-solve with struggling employees before termination becomes necessary.
- Seek creative solutions before instituting layoffs.
- Layoffs are not the fault of the affected employees, and as such, management should take responsibility and show up with compassion and empathy.
- Avoid surprises if at all possible.
- Giving notice equals respect—and dignity—for those affected.
- Building a culture that includes responsible hiring and inclusive problem solving is the best way to prevent layoffs.

Part III

"HUMANING"

Sometimes we get so focused on adulting that we forget humaning. Adulting is getting dressed, sending the mail, making the appointments, running the meetings and the washing machine, making the deals and the lunches. Adulting is stuff we gotta do. But when we only adult we forget why life is amazing—life just becomes one long to do list. So, we gotta remember—while we're adulting: to HUMAN. Humaning is pausing, playing, reading, singing, hugging, laughing, crying, sighing, resting, breathing, forgiving, remembering, sitting, taking a moment out to look and listen and taste and feel. It's when we remember that we're human beings not human doings. Adulting is necessary—but humaning is why we're here.
—Glennon Doyle, Instagram, April 13, 2018

Sometimes, we realize that the life we are living no longer fits our authentic selves, and it is time to shed our proverbial skin so that we may begin again. If you've experienced this, then you know what I mean. It starts as a tiny seed of "what if" and slowly grows inside until it blooms into an undeniable knowing.

It can also be the result of something much more traumatic, such as a house fire, a debilitating illness, or a dramatic change in financial circumstance. Suddenly your old life is no longer possible. The COVID-19 pandemic certainly highlighted the truth that we all handle change differently. The Great Resignation that followed the pandemic is an excellent example of this. Many, after such a scare and confinement, decided that they needed to reengineer their lives, seeking greater freedom or a more satisfying means of making a living. No matter the driver of the change, there are people whom you must tell, and you can be sure your loved ones will have something to say about it.

Some might call it "coming undone," but the radical shift sometimes required to get on your true path can be downright unsettling to those you love. Yet our fealty lies only with ourselves in this big, beautiful life. As such, it is our duty to shift if required, lest we become stuck, bitter, and sad. Telling our loved ones can be tricky, but I am here to help with a few stories to light the way.

Chapter Five

Empty Nester

When the Last Child Leaves

Empty nest is not just about the loud quiet. It's about being at the center of your own life where your kids used to be. You'll be encouraged to embrace your freedom, go back to school, volunteer, but coming first again is not as easy as it sounds. It feels like wearing shoes on the wrong feet. —Susan Bonifant[1]

First off, let's state the obvious: "empty nester" is a horrible term. Is there anything sadder than finding a bird nest with nothing but little broken shells left behind? No wonder so many parents struggle with this stage of life. But what's the alternative? Generations of adult birds all struggling to squeeze into the same small nest? You see where I'm going here.

THE FAIL

Launching into adulthood is a critical juncture in the family dynamic. A failure here means the child doesn't leave the nest and misses the opportunity to become independent. In some cultures, multigenerational living is common and the different generations cohabitate in a loving, productive way. This is not the fail of which I am speaking. I am talking about the parents who infantilize their child and cannot let go or the child who fails to launch into adulthood for a variety of other reasons. In these instances, there is often dysfunction between the parent and child,

65

and external interventions in the form of mental health counseling are required to change the dynamic.

A lighthearted example of this can be found in the 2006 movie *Failure to Launch,* in which Matthew McConaughey plays a thirty-five-year-old boat broker still living at home with his parents. His mom, played by Kathy Bates, makes him breakfast before work every morning, and his dad, played by Terry Bradshaw, is ready to get him out of the house. Because it is a romantic comedy, no real psychological work is done, and the intervention is achieved by a hired love interest played by Sarah Jessica Parker. Although the movie is the emotional equivalent of cotton candy, the issue of failing to launch is a growing problem, according to Dr. Ellen Hendriksen. "Numbers indicate the problem is increasing. . . . [T]he phenomenon is more complicated than simplistic labels might indicate."[2]

There can be many reasons for Peter Pan syndrome, as it is also known, which include economic factors (lack of jobs, student debt, lack of affordable housing), untreated mental health issues, and a declining interest in marriage, which is often a motivator for leaving the nest.

Narcissistic parents often see their children as an extension of themselves and control their lives. The thought of their children becoming independent from them can represent a loss they are unwilling to accept. Social anxiety disorders, video game addiction, and depression can absolutely stop young adults from stepping out on their own, and parents who are codependent might not seek the help that their children need in order to address their mental health issues. It's just easier to keep them at home.

Additionally, in the United States, the cost of health care and the high cost of living relative to minimum wage can be factors preventing treatment from being sought. I know of at least three examples of this personally, and all involved are good people, doing the best they can to deal with the circumstances they are facing. Sadly, something must give in order for change to occur. Eventually, the child of the narcissistic parent will have to find strength through counseling, mentors, or self-help study in order to break away and establish an independent existence. The child with untreated mental health issues eventually either will lose their parents and be forced into independence or become their parents' caretakers. The longer it takes, the harder the launch becomes.

THE BETTER WAY

In my life, my kids were hands-down my top priority. When it was obvious my second (and final) child would be moving out for good, I possessed enough self-awareness to know I was about to become a big hot mess. I imagined myself wandering around my lovely empty nest wondering where my life went. I had done so well when my oldest went to school that I was lulled into a false sense of confidence that I had this shit down. Yet my gut told me that this last one would not be pretty.

Around this same time, I felt a strong pull to be somewhere else—unsure about where, but definitely not where I was. Somewhere deep inside, a seed had sprouted and begun to grow. The seed was an idea, a vision of another type of living that did not require me to be in a place where I was no longer happy. I also knew I needed something to pull me forward through this end-of-parenting life change, like a beacon in the distance on which I could focus. My subconscious began to plan while my conscious self went about the day-to-day of living. At first, I thought this was just a coping mechanism and the idea would go away, but it didn't. Then I thought that it would be a great idea "someday" or "later"—you know—"when the time was right."

Finally, in January 2017, I was talking with my therapist, and this idea of being elsewhere forced its way into the conversation. I really hadn't planned on bringing it up, but my subconscious was getting impatient. Not surprisingly, my therapist pounced on it, asking for myriad details that I did not yet possess. Through this series of questions, I finally gave voice to the specifics. I wanted to sell my beautiful nest, buy a motorhome, and wander until I found a place I didn't want to leave.

There—I said it out loud. I was going to chuck my stable, cushy life for the life of a nomad. After a few probing questions and some internal wrestling, my therapist said, "well, if you are going to do it, you better do it now because of where the real estate market is at." Then it hit me: she was absolutely right. The time was now.

I got to work.

First, I talked to my two sons, who were eighteen and twenty-one at the time. How did they feel about my selling their childhood home? How did they feel about mom becoming a wanderer? Would they feel like I was abandoning them? I have to say, they took it very well. Sure, they said, they would love to keep the real estate in the family, but given the fact that their dad still lived in their hometown, they were not overly concerned with letting go of the house. I am sure it was harder than they let on, but they also wanted to see mom happy, which certainly made the whole thing easier.

Before my decision was final, I connected with two of my dear long-time friends for their input. The first was my former boss, mentor, and true friend Beth. This veteran solo world traveler broke into a huge smile when I timidly told her my idea at our usual Starbucks meetup. She enthusiastically blurted, "I think you should go for it!" *Phew!* What a relief.

Next, I called my friend, Jo, who was living a wandering lifestyle and could share with me the nuts and bolts of my new venture. As expected, she gave me just the encouragement I needed and got me fired up about what was possible.

After that, I had to tell my extended family and friends. The reactions varied greatly. Once they recovered from their initial shock, most reactions fell into one of two categories. The first category consisted of comments like, "By yourself?" "Have you ever camped before?" "Do you know anything about motorhomes?" "Where will you go?" "Aren't you scared? You'll never get back into Carlsbad." The second reaction was along the lines of, "Right on—I'm so happy for you!" "I'm so jealous, take me with you!" After my initial surprise at some of the expressed concern, I learned to enjoy hearing the reactions, because it told me so much about what my friends and family thought about risk taking and life changes.

By the end of February, I held my garage sale, selling some things but giving most of my material possessions away. It was one of the most joyous days of my life. By releasing my stuff, my mental load lightened. I giggled as shoppers walked away with piles of clothes, holiday decorations, sports equipment, video games, etcetera. I mean, I had ten boxes of Christmas decorations alone! Friends and family pitched in, and for their efforts, they received first pick of whatever they wanted. It still makes me smile when I think about it. The rest of the "nice stuff" was given to friends and family when we moved. All that remained was a small storage unit of sentimental items. Most of my photos and kids' art was scanned or photographed and saved to the cloud. Some was sent to a service to be rendered professionally and returned on a thumb drive. It all worked for me.

My house was on the market a few days after the garage sale, thanks to my dear friend, Sans, who is a wonderful realtor. Sans and I had spent five weeks painting and fixing minor details that would make the home ready to sell. My home had never looked better. Three weeks later, the house was in escrow at the full asking price, above market value. It was clear that the universe fully supported this move. Once the decision was made in January, the subsequent pieces fell into place with almost no resistance.

By May, I moved out, ready to buy my home on wheels. I was lucky enough to crash on my best friend's couch (which she obtained from my garage sale) while my boys stayed at their dad's house. That month at Cathy's house was magical; we reconnected like we were in high school. She had just lost her two dogs earlier in the year and was so happy to have my two fur babies, Solo and Castle, staying there. It worked out so well.

During this time, I learned I'd had a motorhome mentor under my nose for years. Upon telling my hilarious "pool guy," Butch, that I would be selling my house, getting an RV, and wandering, he said something to the effect of, "First, I'm really sad I won't see you anymore, but I'm so happy for you! Can I help you shop for your RV?" This guy was a pro and taught me so much! He never once doubted that I could do it. I am so grateful for his presence in my life at just the right time. By Memorial Day, I was packed and on the road in my new home with Solo and Castle.

Fast-forward five years (as of this writing): I am still on the road but now in a smaller, sleeker Sprinter van that my nephew and I built during the COVID-19 pandemic. Both Solo and Castle have crossed over, but before they left, we visited thirty-eight states in the United States and five Canadian provinces—quite a send-off, indeed. They were both changed for the better through our travels, more confident and curious about this beautiful planet we inhabit.

I rescued a new dog named Nellie after her mom died from COVID and I am showing her the ropes of van life. I see my family and friends back home less often, but it is so damn sweet when we are able to get together that it is almost better. Additionally, I have revived old friendships on the road and discovered so many new ones that my cup . . . well, you know.

If you're curious about this way of "humaning," you can see and hear so much more about this ongoing adventure on Instagram

@gerireidsuster. I love answering questions about life on the road because so many people helped me get started when I knew nothing about it except that it was for me.

PREVENTION

For many of us, parenting just happens. We live day-to-day doing the best we can to keep these little humans alive and participating in normal functions. We follow what others do in our community. However, since parenting is absolutely one of the most important roles in life, perhaps we should adopt a better strategy. What if parents developed an eighteen-year plan for each child before birth? Simply the act of doing so (whether or not the plan actually came to fruition) would put parents in the right head space around the changing developmental goals they might have for their child. If you have a partner, it would be a beautiful and enlightening exercise. Start with identifying the hopes and dreams you have for your children.

1. We want them to be authentically themselves.
2. We want them to have loving, lifelong friends.
3. We want them to be self-sufficient by adulthood (assuming no ailments prevent this).
4. We want them to be healthy.
5. We want them to be happy.

Often parents think about these things informally but focus on the wrong things—we want them to be a doctor, a football player, take over the family business, have five kids, etcetera. Rather, we should look at each child as a gift from a magic land: Who are they? What are they going to become? Our role is to support and allow their "becoming," to provide the skills needed to move from sensing their uniqueness to allowing it to flourish during their time here. Ultimately, we need to teach them to thrive without us.

One of my favorite examples of this is Mrs. Gump, played by Sally Field in the beloved movie *Forrest Gump*. Mrs. Gump knows that her son has challenges to overcome and instead of coddling him, she encourages him to face them, adapt, and overcome. Throughout the movie Forrest recounts the many lessons he received from his "Mama." He talks of his leg braces and how his mom called them his "magic shoes" that would "take me anywhere." She teaches him resilience with gems like, "life is like a box of chocolates. You never know what you're going to get." In real life, it is often the parents of children with disabilities who are hyperaware of the need to teach their children these important coping skills from an early age.

There are several great books on parenting and helping your kids develop a growth mindset. If I had it to do all over again, I would read at least one each year—or better yet, listen to it on Audible while running from one sports practice to the next. There are also amazing parenting podcasts that get into specific topics so we can search and find advice from experts just when we need it. If your child is currently struggling, I recommend starting with *The Journey of the Heroic Parent* by Brad M. Reedy. This book helps parents adjust their own perspective before attempting to help their children. Remember, we aren't born knowing how to parent. It is a skill that must be cultivated, and we all make mistakes. The key is to keep evolving.

Finally, when your last child is approaching adulthood, get yourself a plan for *you*! Plan that second honeymoon with your partner. Enroll in the enrichment class you always wanted to take but never had time. Join a running club and sign up for that half marathon. Commit to a big, slightly scary goal to pull yourself through that first year or two as you regain your bearings in this strange new land. Or just sell the nest and hit the road like me! The kids can't move back home if they can't find it.

Chapter Six

The New You—Who Dis?

It matters not what someone is born, but what they grow to be. —
Albus Dumbledore[1]

From the moment we are born, roles are assigned to us by our family,
our friends, and society as a whole. We are seldom allowed the freedom
to explore and become without being inundated by the opinions of others. If those opinions conflict with who we are inside, we often strap a
heaping bag of shame on our back, learn to pretend to be what everyone wants of us, and simply carry on. For some, exiting this externally
imposed persona becomes impossible.

THE FAIL

The fail here is obvious, right? When has pretending to be what others want us to be ever brought true happiness? This struggle is most
obviously and painfully experienced by the LGBTQ+ community.
Discrimination is evil but effective in motivating people to pretend,
conform, and go along with what is deemed acceptable by their family,
community, church, employer, or government. During the past twenty
years, countless stories have emerged of both fathers and mothers coming out as gay after living traditional family roles in order to conform
to societal expectations, to have children they desperately wanted but
didn't think they could have in a same-gender relationship, or simply

to avoid the backlash they would have experienced due to discrimination by those around them. In 2018, the *Washington Post* ran an article titled, "My Dad Lived a Lie. I'm Determined My Kids Won't Have to Do the Same." The author, Jared Bilski, shares that his dad waited until he was on his deathbed to admit that he was gay. Growing up, Jared suspected his father was gay and, after his parents divorced, even confronted him with his suspicions, but his father clung to his denial and the topic was shelved for years. As Jared puts it, "my dad died afraid and ashamed of who he really was."[2] Though this painful lesson now motivates Jared to parent his own children differently, it is a tragedy that such fear of discrimination can cause some to waste their "one wild and precious life."[3]

The discrimination is the fail. The intolerance is the fail. Denial and pretense are the tactics employed for survival and should be met with compassion and support.

To be clear, openly being your true self is not always a safe proposition. Gracefully exiting the expectations of others may not always result in singing "Kumbaya" around a campfire but rather in walking away from a burning bridge.

THE BETTER WAY

And then there was Drew.

I met my friend Drew at the second annual RV Entrepreneur Summit in Fredericksburg, Texas (wine country . . . if you know, you know). We were both gregarious solo travelers and hit it off immediately. He was also a speaker at the summit and promoting a book to which he contributed called *Positive Minded People*. Drew is transgender and shared his journey about how he transitioned and the tough conversations he had with his family. He was so inspiring that I knew I wanted to include his story here.

Drew first came out as gay when he was twenty-one after spending years trying to understand why he was not attracted to men, despite having amazing men in his life. He was out to everyone in his life for seventeen years and dating women exclusively. Yet during that time, Drew became increasingly angry. Something boiled under the surface. He drank, went to bars, and focused on the behavior of others.

A road rage moment at a gas station shook him out of his denial. After a near miss in the parking lot between his car and another, an old white man said under his breath to Drew, "I'm so sick of little bitches like you." In that moment, Drew was ready to fight, but he saw something in the man's eyes that was "serial killer scary." It didn't matter, though, because Drew was raging. As they were facing off, the store attendant came out and Drew yelled to him to call the police because something bad was about to happen.

At that, the old man jumped in his car and drove away. Drew got back into his Jeep, shaking, and thought, "What the hell? If you don't do something, you are going to go to jail or die. You've got to figure this out."

He promptly dove into his search for an answer with his therapist, going within to find out what wasn't working. Around this same time, the Chaz Bono documentary came out about Chaz's gender transition journey in the 2000s. Watching this, Drew clued in to what he was feeling. When he finally faced it, he remembers saying to himself, "Can it just be anything but that?" When I asked Drew why he had that reaction, he said, "Do you want to be the one to tell everyone you are going to change your gender? It's embarrassing and complicated and most people don't understand. Facing that was very, very difficult."

Drew called his mom to tell her he was going to transition from daughter to son. Before she had time to react, he said, "Mom, I was on my own all through being out as gay. You never defended me. I had to defend myself this whole time. I'm not going to survive this without you. I can't do this without you. You're gonna have to step up and be a mama bear. I need you."

"Okay," she said. "I don't know how to do it but okay."

Drew admitted he didn't know what would have happened had she disowned him. "I don't know if I would have survived it, quite frankly," he said. Fortunately, his little sister became his biggest advocate and helped him through it.

Next, Drew moved forward with telling the rest of his family. Drew visited his dad to tell him in person. His dad's response was, "I'm never going to call you anything but [his old name]." Drew's response was, "Well, then it's gonna get real awkward." It took some time for his dad to come to terms with it. Today, they are in a much better place.

Drew was really scared about telling his grandparents. With his sister's support, he visited them in person. When he shared his news with them, they acted like it was fine, probably because they didn't know what to say. "It's still not really a good situation today," Drew says. Some folks are less comfortable discussing things they do not understand and accept.

Drew moved on. He first told friends who he knew would support him and then emailed about thirty people that he felt were the next-level close to him. He sent a survey that said, "Hey, I'm changing my gender. I finally realized what's going on. I'm picking some names. Here's some choices. Will you give me your opinion?" The moment he sent the email, he knew what names he wanted for himself. To his delight, his friends picked the same.

Not everyone will have the same reaction to your decision to change your life as Drew experienced so prepare yourself accordingly.

One of the keys to a graceful exit is finding your squad. These people have your back all of the time, no matter what. It may not be who you expect or want it to be when you start out, but it is critical to have support. Drew advises, "You can't have a gracious exit if you don't have the support to go to when it fucks up. And it's going to. It has to be people that can hold space for you—so not people who are making it about them. A lot of times those are people that are not emotionally connected to you. Sometimes it's people you pay, sometimes it's friends or whatever, but it should only be people that don't want something from you. It should just be about you. You need your Sherpa."

Changes like this require telling your story many times, which is important to anticipate. The more people in your life, the more people you need to tell, which can be daunting at the beginning. Drew had a large circle and realized he couldn't transition quietly. After the survey, he threw himself a birthday party at a bar. Before the party, he made business cards with his new name on it. Every time someone walked into the party, Drew handed the person a card and said, "Hey, I just wanted to let you know I am changing my gender. Here is my new name. The drinks are over there. Have fun."

Drew's strategy was definitely proactive. He approached the communication of his transition like an entrepreneur would deliver an elevator pitch. He took others on his journey and dropped them off but never gave them the opportunity to give their opinions—nor does he want them. Nor are they welcome.

It took him eight months to tell everyone in his life—eight months of repeating the same information, gaining confidence and ultimately compassion for the person on the other side of the conversation. At one point, a relative started to give Drew a hard time when he told him about his transition. Drew said, "Look, I'm giving you information. That's all this is. I'm the same amazing person I was before this phone call and I'll be the same amazing person after. I'm just giving you information that you didn't have and I'm being respectful by doing that. This isn't about you."

Talk about healthy boundary setting!

I asked Drew how he handled it when friends or family slipped and called him by his old name or used the wrong pronouns. He said, "I tell them, 'if you fuck up, just keep going. If you say the wrong name, just keep going, it's okay.' When you are gay or transgender, you have to do it for the rest of your life. It's fucking exhausting."

The fact that Drew was both proactive and empathetic with others eliminated much of the awkwardness during these conversations. That is extremely graceful. He realized that not everyone had experience with what he was going through, nor did everyone know how to respond once they began to learn. As mentioned throughout this book, putting yourself in the other's shoes is an important element of a graceful transition.

Something that Drew helped me to realize is that when we choose to step into another way of living, our natural tendency is to want all of the people in our life to support and join us—at least emotionally. What is more likely, though, is that we're going to lose some people along the way. We may lose touch slowly over time with some and immediately with others because our perceived values are no longer aligned. You have to be okay with that to honor yourself. Also, it's a fallacy to think that you can avoid losing anyone by avoiding change, despite what your heart wants. This underlying assumption that we can prevent exits from happening—that we have control over them—is such bullshit.

"Some doors just shut—you lose people, things, places—and part of you," Drew explained to me. "I was losing myself at the price of not wanting to be that person to embarrass or disrupt my family. I was getting further and further away from myself. I had to say goodbye to the old me. My family had to say goodbye to their sister and daughter and welcome in this new person who is still me but different."

Just as with romantic breakups, sometimes we need to help others absorb news of major life decisions. That can be of great value, but there also comes a point when it no longer serves anyone. Understanding that a "one-and-done" conversation may not work for everyone is helpful when it comes to complex transitions. The goal is to be as gracious as you can, but if the other wants to revisit your decision over and over or attempts to talk you out of it, you have to say, "That's enough. This is about you not wanting to absorb the information I have given you. I have no new information to give, now you need to go do that work on your own."

PREVENTION

In a perfect world, discrimination and intolerance would not exist. Sadly, that is not reality. Each citizen of this human experience can contribute to this solution by rooting out his and her own biases—and yes, we all have them. Every time you find yourself feeling outrage, judgment, or loathing toward another, that is your signal to look within yourself. Your button is being pushed, which means *you have a button*. A button is an unhealed injury, false belief system, or internalized criticism. Again, we all have them. Know thyself and fix thyself are lifelong commandments for graceful living.

The key to preventing the need for "coming out" of the pretense of being anything but your authentic self is to never go *in*—never to hide your light in the first place. If only it were that easy. However, there is an observable trend happening now (to the discomfort of many) with our youth who are being raised by accepting parents. These littles rock their uniqueness. They create their own styles and ways of "humaning" and contributing to the world from an infinite palette.

What about those who are still hiding their light? How do we transition gracefully into the light? First, find your squad, because we all need the sense of belonging provided by our squad. How do you know when you've found it? Brené Brown says it best in *The Gifts of Imperfection*: "Fitting in is about assessing a situation and becoming who you need to be to be accepted. Belonging, on the other hand, doesn't require us to change who we are; it requires us to be who we are."[4] Find where you belong—if not in your own family, then find a new family. There are support groups everywhere. Only those who accept who you are can be a part of your squad.

Second, learn to set boundaries. This magic wand simultaneously keeps out toxic people and reassures your inner child that you are capable of keeping it safe. I had to learn how to set boundaries after my divorce, and it was so helpful in setting the tone for my new coparenting relationship with my ex. The first conversation was the hardest in which I explained that hearing about the new parts of his life without me and our sons was hurtful and not welcome. After that initial boundary definition, it was only a matter of enforcement. Any time he tried to cross that boundary, I simply interrupted with something like, "Okay, back to the kids, what time will you pick them up on Friday?" It was effective, and I felt myself become stronger each time.

Finally, remember that knowing yourself and fixing yourself is a lifelong adventure. There is no destination, just an endless, gorgeous open highway unfolding before you. This is the very work you were sent here to do so, above all, enjoy the ride.

Chapter Seven

Bolt from the Blue

There is nothing permanent except change. —Heraclitus

Whereas some lifestyle or way-of-being changes can be planned or predicted, others sneak up from behind and push you off a cliff you didn't even know was there. Rather than consciously exiting a way of "humaning," a new way is forced upon you. An unexpected medical diagnosis is certainly one such catalyst.

THE FAIL

Perhaps the only thing worse than a diagnosis is a health problem without one. My sister and I grew up for the most part in Southern California during the 70s. We attended public school and my sister struggled in every class except physical education. Every class, every year. The school's solution was to put her in phonetic classes during grade school and, when that didn't work, assign her detention. My parents' solution was endless restrictions for her bad grades and, when they felt that restriction was not enough, beatings with a belt or wooden spoon. Restriction (for those who have never experienced it) meant that she could leave the house only to go to school or to go on family out-ings and it lasted until the next report card was received six weeks later. Same solutions one report card after the next, yet no change in outcome.

The very definition of insanity. When I asked her what school was like for her, the only response was a vehement, "*hell.*"

The "solutions" failed not because she was a willful, uncontrollable child but because she had dyslexia and no one knew. Although dyslexia was first identified in the late 1800s, programs for students with dyslexia didn't emerge in public schools in America until well after my sister quit attending. In order to survive in our household, Kelly adopted unconventional methods of hiding her grades. She learned to alter the paper report cards that were sent home with the students, and then later, when they began mailing them, to intercept them before they fell into our parents' hands. She learned to forge my mom's signature on notes sent home from concerned teachers in order to cover up the fact that she had altered the report cards.

At twelve years old, permanent restriction still in place, Kelly would sneak out of the house at night to find her freedom. She had the will and found her way. The rule-breaking cycle began early—all because of an undiagnosed learning disability. Far worse than all of that was the blow to my sister's self-esteem—at a core level. She could not understand how school was so easy for everyone else and how, despite her trying her hardest, her answers were always wrong. She felt stupid and damaged, and no one tried to help her. All of this led her to make other decisions that changed the course of her life.

When she entered the workforce, she had to work twice as hard to do any tasks that required reading and math. After dropping out of high school, she started a job digging ditches because she excelled at anything physical. After a couple of weeks, her reward for a job well done was a promotion to secretary, where she had to type and file blueprints. She was horrified but needed the money, so she stayed later than everyone else and once paid someone else to type a critical letter for her just to make sure she didn't miss an important deadline. I asked her how she got by and she said, "I just faked it and then started gravitating to leadership roles because I could delegate the stuff that was a struggle for me."

It wasn't until she was thirty-three years old with two children of her own when she took an aptitude test at a local school while searching for a new career path that she learned of her dyslexia. The relief was overwhelming—to finally understand there was a reason. See how a lack of information causes so much unnecessary pain? As a result, we can become trapped in our own type of hell or seek unconventional means for breaking out. Most of the time, these exits are anything but graceful.

THE BETTER WAY

When my son, Jake, was fifteen, he received a diagnosis that changed our lives dramatically: anxiety/depression/suicidal ideation. Prior to this, I recall feeling that something was wrong but rationalizing around his observable changes in behavior. He was a teenager, and at some point their hormones cause them to cross over into what I call "the dark side." Surely that was all it was—just like his brother before him, I just needed to wait for him to come out of it. When he stopped hanging out with his friends, he told me it was because they started experimenting with pot and he wasn't into that. I remember feeling grateful that my son was making good choices for himself, but I later found out that was a lie to get his mom off his back. When he didn't seem to replace his old friend group with new friends, I began to worry but was easily distracted by work, his brother preparing for college, and so on. When he shared with me that he was feeling unmotivated and wanted to find someone to talk to, that got my attention—to an extent.

Part of me felt relieved that he was proactive enough to see his own needs and ask for help, so how bad could it be? (See the rationalization?) I found him a therapist and he went to a few sessions, was given some structure, decided he was good to go, and stopped going.

A few months later, he again came to me and said, "I think I'm depressed." Back to the therapist he went—with greater urgency this time. I will never forget the feeling in my body when she told me that he was suffering from anxiety and depression—a formal diagnosis— and that she wanted to refer him to a psychiatrist for medication. The resistance I felt in my body to those words and that plan of action was shocking. Part of me didn't want it to be true because of what it meant for him. But part of me didn't want it to be true because of what it said about me and my ability to parent and provide the love and security he needed to be happy. My mother-knows-best ego button was being pushed hard. I had to wrestle it as though it were a five-hundred-pound alligator, bringing it back into submission so I could help my child. It is a truly humbling day when you face the fact that your child needs more than you can provide.

How was I to support my amazing son through this process? The first step was to acknowledge that our lives were changed. Then we needed to become students and explorers of our new circumstances. This included reaching out to others for resources and information. That meant we had to tell people—which at first felt awful and shaming—and admit that my son was struggling with mental illness. Although the stigma around such a diagnosis in our culture is lessening, it still exists. As my son's advocate, I imagined a different diagnosis—such as cancer—and realized that we were not going to add shame to this already difficult experience.

With Jake's courageous permission, we told our friends and family exactly what was happening and, as a result, were bolstered by their support as we ventured into the confusing world of doctors, meds, and healing. We were the first in our friend and family group to be so open about what was happening, and I have witnessed a ripple effect in our community that makes me so proud of Jake's courage. Many have reached out to us to ask about Jake's journey, resources, and healing to help with their own struggles around a mental health diagnosis.

I resisted radical measures, whether it be medication or changing his schooling, which was his trigger. I feared that such changes meant crossing some point of no return. I also know now that I was clinging to what I believed to be the only path to happiness for my children: do well in school, go to college, get a good job, and you'll be happy. That was the path most people took, and I feared that any deviation meant I had failed at my single most important job. Then, I watched an incredible Ted Talk by Logan LaPlante, a thirteen-year-old kid whose presentation questioned when the measurement of a good childhood—or life—stopped being health and happiness. That kid brought me to my knees. I realized in one moment that I was focused on the wrong things entirely. Health and happiness were *all* that mattered, and that path could be different for everyone.

Boom. We took Jake out of his high school, sought alternatives, struggling with many but letting him progress at his pace and ability to get back into the world. Jake and I developed new communication patterns that gave him the freedom he needed and me the reassurance I craved. He worked his ass off to crawl out of that dark place and I am proud of how I ultimately showed up for him. Today, he is successfully "adulting," happy and healthy is his new normal, and his diagnosis is something he has learned to proactively manage. I am grateful for this every day.

There is beauty, growth, and purpose in all that life serves us if you look for it—even with bad news. The trick is to shift your focus from fearing what you are losing to curiosity and wonder about what you are gaining. Easier said than done, but it can make all the difference.

PREVENTION

I am not a doctor, so I will not tell you how to prevent an unfavorable medical diagnosis. However, if there is a diagnosis to come, the earlier it is found, the better. Imagine the years of pain my sister Kelly could have been spared if her dyslexia had been diagnosed in elementary school. (The good news is that many school districts are beginning to test students in kindergarten through third grade for dyslexia because it has become the most common learning disability.) In a more general sense, when your child tells you something is wrong, believe them. When your child struggles, give her the benefit of the doubt and look for a root cause. When your body tells you something is wrong, listen and then act.

Another tactic for easing the blow of a sudden diagnosis is to learn to embrace a growth mindset so that when a challenge enters your life, as it most certainly will, it is seen as an opportunity rather than an injustice. Teach your children this as well—you will be amazed at how easily they adopt this outlook. A great book on this for young children is *The Girl Who Never Made Mistakes* by Mark Pett.

What about when the diagnosis is terminal? How does one find beauty and grace when facing the ultimate change in one's "humaning"?

THE FAIL

The honest answer is—many don't. As we have seen in many of the exits discussed in this book, clarity on why the exit is happening and acceptance that the exit is happening are critical to finding grace. For Karen, she resisted both, and her exit was anything but graceful. Karen was a fifty-seven-year-old manager whose identity was tied to her job. She had been experiencing increased exhaustion and when she began coughing up blood, she knew it was time to see a doctor. Never one to go to the doctor on her own, she reached out to the one person she could confide in, my friend Lucy. Karen and Lucy had worked together for years and were close. They spent the next month going to different appointments with different specialists.

And then, Karen had her answer—stage 4 cancer—and she had six months to live. Despite that prognosis, as Lucy put it, "the doctors rolled in with the sales pitch—chemo, radiation, the works." Karen bit and her life became a flurry of work and doctor appointments for the next two months. At this point, she still had refused to tell anyone else about her illness. Her son, her extended family, and her employer knew nothing about her terminal diagnosis. She spent half of the time she had left doing what most of us would put on a list titled "things we hate."

With only a few months to live, Karen started to inch toward acceptance. She made a will. She told her son. And, only because of the numerous appointments that took her away from work, she told her boss. Finally, she told her family.

Karen didn't come from what most would call a warm and loving family. Outside her relationship with her son, on whom she doted, her extended family was not going to show up for her. Lucy tried everything she could to get them to engage and support Karen through this process to no avail. Lucy did her best but Karen's need to control everything meant that Lucy's options were limited.

Karen began taking her prescribed pain medication in the form of fentanyl patches but continued driving her car, showing up to work, and shopping for things she would never use. At work, it was clear something was wrong. Karen nodded off at her desk, had a hard time speaking in staff meetings, and generally scared the crap out of her staff. Karen's boss allowed it because he had promised to keep her diagnosis a secret. No one intervened to say enough is enough. Ultimately, Karen, in her weakened and medicated state, fell and hit her head. This injury eliminated the death-with-dignity option she was planning for her own exit. She never regained lucidity and decisions had to be made for her. She died three weeks later.

I asked Lucy how she would describe the time between diagnosis and death for Karen, to which she replied, "a complete waste of time." Her desire to control everything happening around her prevented her from enjoying the last six months of her life. It is a sad example of the lengths some will go to resist vulnerability.

THE BETTER WAY

I would like to introduce you to my brother-in-law Scott.

Scott is a handsome, six-foot-five, Harley-riding man with a goatee and shaved head. He's an imposing figure who possesses an incredibly kind heart. He began dating my sister when they were both in their forties. They brought into the relationship similar backgrounds and plenty of baggage, the kind that comes from dysfunctional childhoods and the resulting bad choices that haunt you in adulthood. When they began dating, they were both actively working on themselves and on being of service to their community. They dated for six years, slowly letting down walls and learning to meld two strong personalities together, an imperfect but inspiring process. In 2017, they were married under a beautiful olive tree atop a hill at a local park that they could see from their living room window in Southern California.

Despite what we learn from Disney, happily ever after doesn't begin the moment a newly married couple seals their vows with a kiss. The work continues; such was true for Scott and Kelly. They fought for their needs and for each other, always buoyed by love. However, after four years of marriage, there came a moment when it looked like their path forward together might not be viable. Both were beginning to brace themselves for the possibility of a life apart, starting to stockpile emotional bricks for separately rebuilding the walls they had demolished together.

They could feel the exit coming, so they started to plan. As the saying goes, God laughed.

Just days before Kelly was to leave for an extended trip to Utah for some serious soul-searching, Scott was struck by a stomach pain that sent him to urgent care. He was alone when the sonographer gave him the news that something was very wrong. All signs pointed to the possibility of cancer. Scott recorded the conversation on his phone for later listening. When he told Kelly about the appointment, the news didn't immediately compute for her. She had done so much work emotionally to prepare for this relationship sabbatical, working through guilt and fear and then finally choosing to do something radical for herself. Listening to this daunting news felt like a cosmic joke—or worse, some type of trick to force her to stay.

Then she listened to the recording.

Afterward, Scott told Kelly that she should still take the sabbatical, that he could handle this challenge on his own. Kelly wasn't having it. "That's not what we do. That's not what you would do," she said. She immediately canceled the trip.

A few weeks and several medical tests later, the diagnosis was made, and it was the worst possible news: stage 4 cancer, terminal, with no interventions available to improve or extend his quality of life and a prognosis of three to six months to live.

At a moment like this, most of us would cling to denial like a life preserver in a stormy sea. The human mind's ability to protect itself from trauma is so very strong. Many bargain with a higher power for more time. Chasing hope is another tactic, searching far and wide for every possible option to extend life or find a cure. There is another response: accepting the diagnosis as truth and planning how you want to spend the rest of your days.

This was the response that Scott chose. What did it do? It set off a chain reaction of beauty, vulnerability, and healing I have never witnessed before. Scott made it his mission to be the one to tell those closest to him—his mother, sisters, extended family, and large group of friends. Not only did he tell them, but he held space for them as they received the news. The courage he displayed throughout this process allowed him to receive untold blessings—moments of true intimacy, prayers from strangers and loved ones, joy entangled with sorrow that would never have happened had he spread the news through other messengers.

He and Kelly were both gifted with the clarity that such a diagnosis can bring. Their marriage regained full strength—in a heartbeat. They dropped their bricks and moved back toward one another. They quickly made plans to hit the road and maximize their time doing things Scott had planned—you know, bucket list stuff—but hadn't gotten around to doing. Their travel was effortless, and they were gifted with magic in the form of plans working out, storms tiptoeing around their reservations, and fall colors showing up at just the right moment. Other humans came forth to facilitate, adding magic to their journey with free stays and spontaneous plane rides. Without resistance, magic is given a seat at the table, and joy is her plus one.

Was it easy? It should be clear by now that exits are never easy— even graceful ones. There were moments of extreme stress, fear, frustration, and doubt, along with ever-changing expectations about what was possible and how much time was left. This shit is hard, no matter what path one chooses. I will take hard intermixed with breathtaking beauty, love, and joy every time. I encourage us all to set our intentions to be as courageous and generous when faced with our own expiration date. There will be no regrets for Scott when he steps out of his human vessel a happy man, deeply in love and soars on to his next adventure.

I had the extreme honor of interviewing Scott about this journey in January 2022. Here is a peek at our conversation.

Have friends shied away from facing your diagnosis, because it's too scary for them to face or accept?

I found a lot of people can't handle it. They can't face it and they can't accept it. I was surprised by how many people are struggling with this. I made it clear that it wasn't just about me. This whole process is affecting everybody who knows me. It's not just about me, so that was pretty eye opening.

Did it make you feel bad when people couldn't engage after your diagnosis?

No, it didn't hurt my feelings. I see it as levels of acceptance, just like levels of evolution. We're able to accept certain facts, but there are some things we can't even accept into our reality. It's an indication of where they are at. I'll be conscientious about it, and I'll say, "Look, now is not a good time, but if you find later on, say, 2:00 in the morning, you wake up and want to ask a question, feel free because I'm totally okay talking about this deal and it may help you in the future going through it with someone else." Unfortunately, I've been around a lot of people who have died myself, and each time there were new revelations for me to come to terms with.

You have the unique perspective of having experience on both sides, watching loved ones dying and facing your own. Is it scarier to be on this side or watching it happening to someone you love?

What I've noticed in the people I've been close to who have passed is that their loved ones weren't accepting it and were in torment about it. To me, that is the scariest part, because they are not accepting of the reality, and it's torture for them to deal with. I know their loved ones that are passing don't want to see or feel that. There's only been a couple of times I've seen it with the person dying, and they were dealing with almost a rebellion to the truth. That is like their own personal hell. That's to me the scary part. Thankfully, I haven't experienced that yet, and I don't know if I will.

When part of my family heard this news, they did not want to accept the fact. They are still struggling with it. Some of my very close friends are still struggling with it. I feel a very big sadness for them, because I understand it as a torture. It's a fact that I am dying. I don't want to, don't get me wrong, it's not something I'm looking forward to. There's never been a point in time where I didn't believe it was true. There's never been this false hope that I'm gonna beat this. I've had this level of trust for the information that I've been given all along and I'm very, very grateful for that. It has allowed me to pick up and make better decisions throughout my days about what I want to do and how I want to feel today. So, the resisting the truth is the scary part.

What blessings have you received that you wouldn't have otherwise received if you weren't dying?

Well, the first thing that comes to mind is Kelly. Kelly and I, in a lot of ways, are like oil and water. We have such strong wills, and our relationship has not been an easy one. But we've both been committed first and foremost to some kind of spiritual seeking. We don't know what it is. We don't know what God is, we can't define what God is, but I know that both of us have been very much in realization that there is something greater than us. We're pretty powerful people, both of us. Individually we can move mountains; we can make shit happen individually. That creates a challenge and a struggle for us. Both of us got to a point where we realized that we were broken, and we needed divine help and we didn't know where to go to get it. So, we've both been on this path of trying to find it, trying to seek it, risk all to obtain it.

So, along the process, it's been a very big challenge for us to stay together. At some points, we haven't. When I heard this news, I realized that was an option perhaps she should entertain, and she said, "Oh no, that's not what we do." She looked at me and added, "That's not what you would do. That's not what we would do."

I'll tell you what: hearing this news solo might have been so much easier if it was just me I had to worry about. But, my God, having her at my side, I've learned and grown so much. I've learned so much about actual intimacy, actual trust, actual commitment, that I didn't even know was fucking possible. I've never known anyone stronger than Kelly. She flipped a switch and she's been relentless. She has been this powerhouse that is so full of love. The small things go away. Truth, intimacy, levels of trust . . . we have bonded like a whole person I never knew was even fathomable.

In addition to Kelly, the rewards have been like having a fifty-five-gallon drum poured over you constantly. It's like standing under Niagara Falls. They have been pouring in on us like you can't imagine. I could give you example after example. You don't see those kinds of blessings normally. You go through life kind of like a pinball bouncing off bumpers. You don't really acknowledge things. But there are these things that are showing up in my life and slapping me in the face because of this news. I've received phone calls from people who have said, "I'm struggling with this. Can I come by and see you?" And I've been able to sit with them and talk for hours. It's just been unbelievable, the amount of blessings we've had. Kelly and I were open to receiving and acknowledging every blessing along the way. We would wake up and look at each other and say, "This is happening right now; how is this happening?"

What do you wish for your friends and family?

Happiness, joy, not a moment of sadness. Not a moment of regret. I don't want any regret.

Do you have regrets?

I think I've pretty much covered my regrets. If there are any left, maybe the time wasted on sorrow, pity, and self-absorption. Because there is so much beauty. I could remember, right over on that hillside, a moment after 2005. I would watch the sunrise as I was selling newspapers on that street corner. It dawned on me, "Wait, the sun has been rising every day of my life. Why have I just now been noticing it?" There is a regret to that, but at the same time, I can do it now. Instead of regretting that I didn't realize it in the past, I'd rather just appreciate it now. So that's what I wish for everybody who is left behind. Pay attention; see it now. You can see beauty in everything. Look for it, and I guarantee you it's there—even in your worst challenge. That's a guarantee.

*With every death, there is usually at least one person left behind who
is stuck in grief over the person who died. What would you say to that
person?*

"I'm fine. I'm fine." That's what I would say.

Had I heard this news before I turned forty years old, I would not have
been fine. My perspective has changed to the point where I'm 100 percent satisfied with my life. I don't regret even some of the worst things
I've done, because they've allowed me to experience these last seventeen
years. And they have been game changing. I've been able to reach people
I never thought I could reach. I've been reached by people I never knew I
could be reached by. I've lived my life full of joy. That's what I want for
everybody. Remember the good times we've had, and remember nothing
but joy is worthy of having in our hearts. Our hearts are supposed to be
filled with love, so let's do that.

What do you want Kelly to know as she faces life on her own?

That I appreciate everything that she's done for me. That I appreciate her
sticking with me, that she's got this, that she deserves this. And that she
deserves to be happy and free and enjoy life. I want her to just absolutely
enjoy and appreciate her every moment. Be free of sorrow, depression,
resentments, fears, insecurities. I wish she could see herself like I see
her. She's such a beautiful soul who can do anything and deserves everything. I just wish for one moment she could see herself through my
eyes, because she is the most beautiful human being I have ever come
into contact with. And it's been such an honor to walk this path with her.
I love you, baby.

PREVENTION

Whenever a centenarian is interviewed, they are inevitably asked, "To
what do you attribute your longevity?" The answers are as varied and
hilarious as you might imagine. Some swear by a daily glass of whiskey
while others credit their love of salsa dancing. In other words, no one
can tell you how *you*, specifically, can prevent a life-changing diagnosis. We all have to die of something.

What I can say is eat your vegetables and strive to live a life that
brings you joy—whatever it takes. I used to listen to the *Dr. Laura Program* on the radio as a way of building tolerance for opposing views.
One of the most impactful questions that she asked her callers who were

clinging to something or someone that clearly made them miserable was, "Between now and dead, is this how you want to live your life?" Asking this type of question, at regular intervals, is an effective tool for gaining clarity. If the answer to that question is an emphatic *no*, then it is time to "get busy living, or get busy dying."[1]

THE BLUEBERRIES

If, at this point, you still do not understand what I mean by blueberries, I applaud you for reading this book in the order you require, and I love that "humaning" is your first priority. In a nutshell, blueberries represent the good stuff or key learnings from the chapter. Check out the end of chapter 2 for the full explanation.

- Understand the difference between "adulting" and "humaning," and strive for balance between the two.
- Know thyself and fix thyself—it is a lifelong practice.
- Find your belonging and cultivate your squad.
- Keep your spiritual/relationship house clean so that if a diagnosis occurs, precious time won't be spent addressing "old business".
- Fight the urge to sink into denial, to gather facts and second opinions, and then search within to find your own truth because time is your most precious resource.
- Be transparent with loved ones during your journey—it allows everyone to more quickly support you.
- Do not put off your dreams—strive for balance between making a living and truly living, because tomorrow is not guaranteed.

Part IV

"UN-HUMANING"

Death is not the opposite of life, death is the opposite of birth. . . .
[D]eath happens not to you but to an experience you are having.
—Dr. Deepak Chopra[1]

"Un-humaning" is the shedding of our physical form and the exit of what remains from this lifetime. It is the end of our experience here. Some believe there is nothing beyond this one human experience while others believe there is everything. I believe it is a gorgeous mystery that awaits us all when our time here as humans concludes. No matter what you believe or what we call it, the truth is that every human experience will come to an end.

We all know this from an early age, but few of us really embrace the truth that it will happen to us. It is a far-off concept that, unless you are old and can feel your expiration date approaching, most of us would rather not think about—much less develop a plan around. I am not asking that we all embrace death or begin discussing our mortality frequently. I am, however, suggesting that we move beyond denial. When your time approaches, or that of a loved one, you can stand courageously in that truth so you may create a graceful exit from this plane. I realize this is asking much, but the payoff is everything to those involved.

Chapter Eight

All Creatures Great and Small

How lucky I am to have something that makes saying goodbye so hard. —Winnie the Pooh[1]

Although pets are not human, their loss can be one of the first we experience in life and, for some, one of the most devasting. When I was in grade school, I was required to write an autobiography and bind it into a little book with wallpaper on the cover. In my little book, there was a chapter on pets. Reading it some thirty-seven years later, I was astonished at the number of pets I had—and lost—during my first twelve years on the planet. When I added up all of the kittens, dogs, and birds, I had twenty-three family pets in twelve years! It was quite disconcerting to read my twelve-year-old self matter-of-factly describing one lost pet after another, many that had run away, some that had been given up due to a change of circumstances, and a few that died prematurely because of predators. Not one of my pets died of old age. We were clearly terrible pet owners.

As a result, I was exposed to pet loss early and often in my life. I grieved each little soul when it left, and no one attempted to hide the harsh truth from me. The circle of life was real to me long before the Disney movie and catchy theme song came into existence. However, that is not always the case, as my dear friend Cathy's adventures in parenting illustrates.

THE FAIL

It is especially important to prepare yourself for the passing of pets, because they usually have a shorter lifespan than we humans. However, like the topic of exits in general, few of us really prepare for this certainty.

Cathy is blessed with four children. While at a pet food store with her youngest son, Davis, they noticed an enclosure with small gray feeder mice, sold as both pets and as food for large snakes. Horrified by the thought of these cute creatures being swallowed by snakes, Cathy and Davis decided to save one of the mice. They brought it home as Davis's first pet. Unbeknownst to them both, the tiny creature, "Lil Man," would be the first of many Lil Mans. Nowhere in the process of choosing and bringing home Lil Man did they discuss lifespan.

Inevitably, the day came when Cathy checked Lil Man's cage, only to find that he had expired. Davis was not at home, and she absolutely did *not* want to talk about death with him at such a young age. So what's a mom to do? You can guess what's coming next: she rushed out to purchase an identical mouse to avoid sharing the bad news. Davis was none the wiser (interesting phrase, *none the wiser*).

We've seen this story line depicted on TV and it's very funny. However, my dear friend repeated this process *four* times! On the final time, the family was away on vacation and Cathy's sister Trish was pet sitting. Poor Trish went to three different pet stores in a panic before she found a mouse that closely resembled Lil Man in appearance.

When Cathy came home from vacation and we were catching up on each other's lives, she told me the story of all five Lil Mans. It dawned on me as we laughed through tears that by hiding the "circle of life" from her kids, Cathy was missing out on the opportunity to teach them about death when the stakes were relatively low. How awful would it be if the first time they experienced death was that of a close family member, such as a grandparent? I pointed this out and she had a big aha moment. When the fifth and final Lil Man crossed over, she told Davis the truth and he took it very well.

THE BETTER WAY

Pets hold a special place in our lives because they offer love uncon-ditionally and are a constant presence. Once they have passed, their absence can be crushing. As I shared earlier, pets have been a part of my life since I was in elementary school. However, one pet in particu-lar stole my heart. His name was Bear and he was a gorgeous blend of Labrador and rottweiler. He was a unique caramel color with a big rott-weiler head and white markings. He had a habit of grabbing my leg with his front paw to get me to play with him. He was bright, curious, and loved me so completely that I could not help but fall for him. Sadly, our love affair was destined to be brief, because he became ill with a rare blood disorder at age three. After many treatments and a brief recovery, he fell ill quickly, and in a matter of days was critical. I was faced for the first time with the decision about whether it was time to let him go. This seemed an impossible choice that I did not want to make.

Bear's medical team was so helpful in guiding me through this pro-cess, as was my dear sister Kelly. Once I came to understand that he would not recover and that his death would be painful without interven-tion, I made the only choice that made sense for my sweet Bear. I called my sister and asked her to pick up my two sons and our other dog, Solo, to give them an opportunity to say goodbye. This is an important part of a graceful exit—allowing loved ones to say goodbye if possible. That includes other pets. My boys, who were about ten and thirteen at the time, came into the room where Bear was resting, followed by my sister Kelly and Solo. They all spent a few moments loving on our sweet Bear while still processing the shock that it was happening so quickly. Solo licked Bear's face, so sweetly attentive that it nearly broke my heart in two. When it was time, Kelly took the boys and Solo back to the waiting room, and I held that enchanting creature's face as the kind veterinarian quietly put him to sleep.

After Bear was gone, we brought Solo back into the room at our vet's suggestion so that he would understand what had happened. Solo did not even look at Bear. He knew instantly that the essence of his friend was no longer in the room. He immediately walked to the door that opened to the outside of the building as though he could not get out of that room fast enough.

I, on the other hand, cried more immediately and harder with this loss than I had for any other, human or canine. Perhaps it was because his life was cut short, but I also think he showed me a glimpse of that perfect, sweet love we are all seeking at a time in my life when I questioned whether such a love could exist. What made his exit more graceful was that we faced it together as a family, said our goodbyes together, and kept him in our memories forever. Yes, it was a very hard day, but we are all the wiser for staying present in the moment and going through it together.

PREVENTION

Although there is no preventing death, we can do our best to stop denying the existence of death. For adults, this should be obvious. However, some recalibrating may be in order for those of us who were raised by parents who never talked about death and have yet to experience a loved one's death personally. One of the best methods for facing the concept of mortality—in addition to reading this book—is to talk about it. Ask people who have experienced death what it was like, how they faced it, how they moved on, and what to expect. Knowledge is power.

I am also a big fan of the overlapping pet strategy. The idea is to introduce a new pet as the current pet nears the end of its lifespan. This practice has multiple benefits. First, the current pet trains the new pet on the ways of the home through example. I have seen this happen with each dog I have known that overlapped with an established dog in the home. It can also lessen the blow when the first pet crosses over. For some, especially the elderly, their pet is their only companion, and when their pet passes, their reason for living can pass with it. If you know of someone who has just lost a pet, at a minimum, check in on him. If possible, take him to a local shelter to pick out a new companion and save a life.

Another tool is to practice living in the now with your pet so that you're soaking up life as it happens. Make memories with your pet, have adventures, celebrate birthdays, or wear silly costumes. The joy your pet exudes is contagious! Finally, a consistent gratitude practice serves as a reminder of how precious life is, including all your favorite beings.

Even animals that are not our pets deserve a graceful exit. This lesson was taught to me by my son, on what we now refer to as possum Thursday. Many years ago when sweet Bear was still alive, he brought a possum into our house one morning before school. Upon inspection, it was immediately clear that this possum was not doing well. I was pretty sure it wasn't going to make it. My son Jake, on the other hand, was quite certain it *was* going to make it. He quickly informed me that it was our duty to ensure this creature had the help it needed.

Now, to be clear, I come from a family who saw pets as pets, not as family members. Remember, we went through twenty-three pets in twelve years. They were there for our pleasure and had to be low maintenance in order to remain with us. Possums and other vermin were not even considered.

My first instinct was that we needed to, you know, bury it—circle of life and all that. Period. When I shared this with my son, he was visibly horrified. He quickly set me straight by asking me, "What makes *this* life any less valuable than, say, Bear's life? Or my life?" Wow! Did I mention he was ten? What do you say to that? I mean, my son just held me to a higher standard for a possum covered with fleas and bugs. I didn't even know how to begin in terms of saving this creature's life. It's moments like this that motherhood really screams for a tropical island—or at least a cocktail.

Well, I am proud to say that I rose to the challenge set by my son and found the nearest wildlife rescue center. It was open that Thursday. I took the possum in a box to Project Wildlife, handed him over, and paid my $20 donation.

I thought it was all behind me until the very next Thursday, when another possum was found in my yard not doing so well. It appeared that Bear had chewed on it a bit, perhaps in transit, but had no real interest in consuming the poor thing. Once again, I took a possum to Project Wildlife and coughed up a second donation for their service. The following Thursday, we had, believe it or not, a *third* possum brought to us by our dear dog. And for a third time, with great trepidation, I traveled to Project Wildlife. The people there were beginning to think I was a bit of a freak, even suggesting that I clean out the "possum nest" in my backyard. All I could do was laugh.

What I realized later was that the universe was testing my commitment to the higher standard that my son had inspired me to reach. By testing me three weeks in a row, it really brought home that message and lesson. As a result, I am now compelled to do whatever I can for injured animals, critters, and even insects, because my son taught me that all life has value. The most graceful thing one can do might sometimes be anything possible to avoid an exit from happening at all.

Chapter Nine

When Main Characters Leave

What we have once enjoyed we can never lose. All that we love deeply becomes a part of us. —Helen Keller[1]

When I was a child, death was not discussed in my family. With the exception of one hamster that ate the other and a gruesome dogs-eating-kittens incident, pets generally just disappeared.

Thus, my first memory on the topic was the sudden death of my step-grandmother. I had met this woman only a few times and she did not live near us, so the blow was light for me. For this I am thankful. However, her death made an impact, perhaps because I hadn't really applied the concept of death to anyone in my life. My stepfather's reaction definitely unsettled me, and I recall the world feeling slightly less safe and life a bit more serious. The idea that someone could be permanently erased from my life was hard to grasp and not something for which I had been prepared. Of course, because I was a young child and my family tended to avoid painful discussions, my questions and reactions were not addressed. Someone quickly changed the subject.

THE FAIL

Clearly, the hardest exit to face is the final exit—for those we love, for those we admire, and our own. An especially difficult scenario is when someone you love with whom you have unresolved issues dies unexpectedly. We tend to think that we always have more time. If one's time is up before all parties are ready, or at least emotionally "clean," the result can be an exit without peace, leaving survivors struggling with guilt and regret.

Another tough scenario is when you believe you are cool with your loved one, only to find after her passing that perhaps you were not. Something like this happened to me with my father. Pops left when I was eighteen months old—actually, my mother left him. I do not recall this exit, of course, but he left my everyday life as a result of that divorce. He picked up my sister and I for birthdays and Easter some-times. As I recall, we saw him two or three times a year. As I became an adult, we grew closer, although we never had the typical father/daughter relationship. When Pops died at the age of fifty-four from heart failure, my sister Kelly and I had zero warning. He was home alone, watching the San Diego Padres lose to the St. Louis Cardinals in game three of the National League playoffs in 1996. I think the game did him in; he was a huge Padres fan. In the days and weeks that followed, I thought back to our last conversation before he died. We had laughed and said our "I love you's," which brought me peace. However, when my sister and I were going through the will and probate process after his death, we discovered that he had recently removed me as a beneficiary from his retirement fund. This was unusual, because every other asset was split equally between my sister and me.

Later, a family friend told me Pops changed it because he was upset with me about something that had happened a few years before between my sister and I. *Ouch*—what am I supposed to do with that? I had no way of confirming this story nor of resolving the feelings of hurt this message caused. Prior to hearing the supposed reason, I had assumed the best about Pops' intentions, thinking he wanted to give my sister a bit more because she was a single mom at the time. I was fine with this and at peace with his decision. However, hearing this secondhand explanation left me feeling anything but peaceful about my relationship with my dad—all because it was too late to clear the air. Not what I would call graceful.

Another fail scenario involves my first experience with the death of someone close to me. Growing up, my mom had a group of lovely and amazing friends, which had been together since grade school. They came to be known as "the Ladies." These women were tight and a bit crazy. Imagine the Ya-Ya's from Rebecca Wells's novel *Divine Secrets of the Ya-Ya Sisterhood* but set in a San Diego County beach community in the 1970s. They had been through everything together—first loves, heartbreak, marriages, divorces, babies, remarriages, death, and so on. To this day, the remaining members of the Ladies—now in their eighties—drink tequila, have slumber parties, and take road trips on a regular basis. The unofficial leader of this zany band of gorgeousness was a tall, lovely creature named Joyce, one of my mom's dearest friends. Although we were unrelated, I grew up calling Joyce "Auntie." Her children will always be my cousins.

Just after "the Ladies" celebrated Joyce's fiftieth birthday in Aruba, Joyce became very ill and was hospitalized. She was diagnosed with advanced lung cancer, although she hadn't smoked in years. Despite their shock and devastation, my mom and the rest of the Ladies rallied, as they are known to do. They brought all kinds of fun and magic to their sweet Joyce and did their best to make her laugh.

One day, my mom asked if I wanted to go to the hospital to visit Joyce. I froze. This was a woman whom I loved and admired on many levels. She threw my twenty-first birthday party at her beautiful home and created a magical night I will never forget. She was a role model in business and a leader in a male-dominated industry. As someone new to the business world starting to develop a knack for leadership, I admired everything she did.

I will never forget the time I ran into her on an airplane—we were on the same flight heading to the East Coast. It was my first solo business trip, and I was a tad unsure of myself at the time. When Joyce saw me from her seat as I boarded the plane, she flagged me down and sweetly arranged with the other passengers for me to sit next to her. On the flight, she asked about what I was doing in my new position and gave me much-needed advice and confidence. She was my fairy godmother, and I just couldn't imagine her no longer being with us.

I did not go to the hospital. My fear of death—more specifically, my fear of her death—anchored me to my home and my usual routine. I supported my mom and sent my love with her, but I simply could not go. Before I knew it, Joyce was gone, and it was too late to change my mind.

I failed to tell Joyce how much she meant to me. I failed to say good-bye, which haunted me for years. It was not the graceful exit I would have liked to have had with her, but a valuable lesson that allowed me to show up differently for others in the future. For that I am grateful, because the stakes were about to go up.

THE BETTER WAY

Twelve years after Auntie Joyce crossed over, my sweet mom, Char, joined her. When mom was diagnosed with lung cancer—less surprising, because she smoked for more than forty years—we knew she was in for a fight. When we met with the oncologist, he was positive and full of hopeful platitudes. After the visit, I called the doctor to clarify my mom's prognosis, because my gut told me to ask more directly without my mom in the room. His demeanor was completely different. "She has about six months to live," he stated bluntly. I was floored by the doctor's candor, though I somehow knew this was coming.

The next two weeks were a flurry of appointments and emotions. Our "team"—mom, her husband Dave, my sister Kelly, and I—formulated a plan. Mom would focus on getting better and Dave would help her with food and supplements. Kelly would be her medical advocate, and I would handle communication with family and friends. Our discussions were hopeful and optimistic, yet I knew somehow that my mom was planning her exit. I found the process scary and distinctly different from the process with my dad. With warning, the opportunity to address unresolved issues was available, but I found that many of her friends and family members seemed too afraid to go there. Often, they focused on hope for a cure or treatment or their thoughts about how Char looked that day. It was as though no one wanted to acknowledge that there was another possible outcome.

On one hand, this was practical and made sense. When I had the opportunity to have honest conversations with my mom about the "what-ifs," she seemed relieved to be able to plan and begin to accept the idea for herself. It was as if we had a secret pact to maintain optimism with the rest of the family, but she and I could discuss, grieve, and plan for her reality. There was such beauty in being able to do this. For me, it helped to answer the big scary questions like, Was she afraid? Did she feel like anything was left undone or unsaid? Knowing she was at peace with the life she had lived was such a relief. Yet as the reality of what approached settled onto my shoulders, I had a few moments of panic when I wanted to run away and pretend none of this was happening. I held fast to the advice given by my dear friend, Beth: "Geri, all you have to do is show up. The rest will take care of itself."

She was so right. It didn't matter if I didn't know what to say or how to help in each moment. What mattered was that I was there, involved and emotionally present for these terrifying but important events. Having learned the impact of not showing up with my Auntie Joyce, I was motivated to be brave and face my mother's transition.

That made all the difference. I learned how to sit with my dying mom and how to talk to her about the end. She still had a positive outlook, but she was also able to speak with me about what she wanted to happen after she was gone. She confided how difficult it was for her to accept all the love coming from family and friends all over the country each day. She could not express enough appreciation for the meals delivered by her brother-in-law Dan and his lovely wife Sue. When her niece's kindergarten class made a butterfly mobile with wishes for her good health, written by each tiny hand, she was forced to face her own beliefs about her worth. Just as I had to stand in my fear of losing her, she had to stand in her fear that she was not worthy of this outpouring of love. The beautiful thing is, she stood tall.

For some people, receiving is so incredibly hard, whether it be a simple compliment or unconditional love. This type of person can never give enough. To others, it appears to be their life's mission, but when the tables are turned and they are forced to receive, how they squirm! This describes my mother. Because she was dying, she was in no position to sidestep their love. We had a wonderful conversation about this in which she shared that the outpouring was difficult for her to handle. I reminded her that in accepting their offerings, she was giving them peace after she was gone. I also sang her a few lines from one of my favorite songs, John Mayer's "Wheel," which suggests that the love we put out into the world will someday return to us.

Something in Mom appeared to shift after that conversation. She seemed to accept what was coming with less doubt and more grace. When she passed, she knew how well and how greatly she was loved, as well as the positive impact she made on those around her. It was enough. For my part, I can look back on how I showed up with few regrets. Nothing important was left unsaid. I did my best and I'm at peace with how I showed up for her and for myself.

One of the most beautiful stories I have encountered about a family's ability to orchestrate a graceful exit comes from the final days of a beautiful four-year-old boy named Ethan Van Leuven from West Jordan, Utah. Ethan had been living with leukemia for two years but was no longer responding to treatment. In October 2014, doctors gave Ethan days or at most a couple of weeks to live. Instead of becoming paralyzed by this impossibly short window, Ethan's family decided to pack maximum life and celebration into the time he had left. Their friends, family, and neighbors responded in kind. The next week was filled with celebrations of holidays and birthdays that Ethan would miss. They dressed up, trick-or-treated, and celebrated Christmas with decorations and gifts. Ethan even rode on a fire truck. The police told him that he was their hero.

The staggering outpouring of love for this little boy reflects the absolute best of what humans can do when they rise in the face of adversity. His parents put aside their own fear and grief to ensure that their son's final days were as special and magical as possible. It is one of the most stunning examples of creating a graceful exit that I can imagine. To learn more about Ethan's story, visit www.littleethanvanleuven .blogspot.com.

PREVENTION

"Keep your spiritual house clean" is one of the best pieces of advice I can give to those wanting to prevent an ungraceful exit. Clean up misunderstandings as they happen and express your love and appreciation loudly and often. Celebrate the small moments and live with daily gratitude. All of these things contribute to a clean spiritual home. When exits happen, strive to live in truth, stay out of denial, and fully experience these events and all the pain, joy, and growth that comes with them. According to Elisabeth Kubler-Ross, author of *On Death and Dying,* "Those who have been immersed in the tragedy of massive death during wartime, and who have faced it squarely, never allowing their senses and feelings to become numbed and indifferent, have emerged from their experiences with growth and humanness greater than that achieved through almost any other means."[2]

When we stay in denial, we miss the experience. This "conscious" approach lessens the psychological impact of these events so that we may learn from them and move through them, without getting stuck in the pain they cause.

In terms of creating a graceful exit from this life, I would be remiss if I did not say a few words about hospice. My mom was fortunate enough to be delivered into hospice care during her final weeks of life. It was one of our greatest blessings. Shortly after arrival, Mom was settled into her bed in a gorgeous room with a balcony that overlooked Mission Valley in San Diego. On a clear day, you could see the Pacific Ocean. Mom thought she was in a beautiful resort.

One day, a tall male nurse with a sweet smile walked in. He approached my mom with something close to reverence. His name was Jerry, and he asked my mom if there was anything he could get for her. Her huge eyes looked up at him from her emaciated little body, and she said in a tiny voice, "I would really love a beer."

Without missing a beat, Jerry asked, "With or without ice, Char?"

I didn't think my mom's eyes could get any bigger but they did. Her smile was huge. After Jerry brought her a Miller Lite, her favorite, she took two grateful sips before falling into a deep sleep. It was a tiny moment of grace I will never forget.

Before that experience, I was unfamiliar with hospice and the many services it provides. The hospice movement dates back to AD 1000, its intention to offer an integrative approach to complement and even take over medical treatment when everything medically possible has been done for the dying. In 1967, Dame Cicely Saunders updated the hospice movement when she opened St. Christopher's Hospice in London, where she questioned the idea that people had to die in agony. Instead, the focus was on palliative care, with the intention of keeping the dying stable both spiritually and physically.

In his podcast called "Working," David Plotz interviewed hospice nurse Cathy Gruser, who discussed the day-to-day aspects of her job.[3] In addition to the obvious care like feeding and bathing, the hospice worker also provides pain management. This can include spiritual as well as physical pain. If the patient is able to talk, the hospice worker can lead her through something called a "life review," asking the patient about her life—"Where are you from?" "What did you do in life?" This can lead to deeper conversations during which the patient opens up about concerns for family or fears about dying. Being able to share these feelings is an important part of the exiting process. Finally, the hospice worker helps family members focus on what to say to their loved ones, steering them away from judgment and helping them focus on love and reassurance. With this deft guidance from the angels at hospice, families are often able to create an exit that is filled with less angst and more love.

Chapter Ten

I Did It My Way

For life and death are one, even as the river and the sea are one.
—Khalil Gibran[1]

Death can be an unsettling truth to face, but it is the one certainty we all share in this human experience. So why is it that we don't talk about death, or plan for it, or celebrate it? I am often surprised when others are shocked by how openly I discuss death—either in telling a story or talking about my parents, who died relatively young. I don't usually describe them as deceased in whispered tones. I usually just state, "they are dead" . . . because they are. It is simply an accurate description of their current physical state. I am not disrespecting them by saying it this way.

The tendency in our culture to speak of the dead in flowery phrases says everything about the comfort level of the survivor and very little about the deceased person. Obviously, there is much fear here, but often we avoid this topic because we are concerned about how others will react. It is taboo in American culture to discuss and face death head on. Unless you are a hospice worker, it is not a part of our common dialogue.

THE FAIL: THE UNTHINKABLE

If talking about death is hard, imagine talking about death by suicide. It takes the reality of "hard" to a whole new level. This type of exit is layered with an emotional complexity intensified by the religious, spiritual, or cultural beliefs of surviving loved ones. When loved ones die as a result of illness, accident, or old age, they are often remembered through a golden filter. They are revered, faults are forgotten, and fondest memories are played on a loop in survivors' minds. When a loved one dies by suicide, though, no such filter is in place. Words such as "selfish" might be used. This difference is really a reflection of our struggle to understand this type of exit. I am heartened to see a shift toward breaking this taboo and discussing the topic of suicide with greater compassion and understanding.

So is there a way to make death by suicide a graceful exit?

The honest answer is: I am not sure. There may be ways to make it slightly less painful, but because there is the element of choice in this type of death, the pain, anger, guilt, and confusion of survivors will always be greater than with death by some other means.

For me, grace is found in breaking the taboos surrounding mental illness. Then we can talk more openly about death by suicide as a possible outcome with certain mental illness diagnoses. It comes from supporting parents who have lost children to suicide by remembering their children, speaking their names with loving fondness, and listening to the parents do the same. Grace comes from talking to our loved ones about mental health and devoting time to our own. It comes from role modeling good mental health practices for others, just as we would physical health.

If you are reading this book in order to figure out how to exit by suicide without hurting anyone, I'm sorry, but that's just not going to happen.

Here is what I want to say to you: *I am so very sorry you are in so much pain.* I cannot know what you are feeling, but I can share what I've learned by talking to people who have survived losing loved ones to suicide. Here is what we would say to you:

- Stay
- Fight
- Ask for help
- Find a doctor
- Go back to your doctor
- Get medication

- If your medication is not working, ask your doctor to change it. Or find a new doctor if yours is not helping you.
- You are loved and valued, no matter what this moment, day, or week feels like.
- Call (800) 273-8255 (TALK), the US National Suicide Hotline. If outside the United States, visit www.iasp.info.

DO EVERYTHING YOU CAN TO STAY

Now, more specifically, here are some difficult things I learned from my friend, Amanda, who lost her sweet brother Gregory to suicide. After her brother's death, Amanda was gutted, and it dramatically changed her life. In order to process how he died, she immersed herself in learning everything she could about this manner of exit. She then shared what she learned bravely and openly with loved ones and on social media. We spoke at length about her experience and journey, and she was kind enough to allow me to share it here. This is what you need to know if you feel this type of exit is your only option.

When there is a suicide, the family has to clean up any physical mess left behind. I'm not talking about unpaid bills or parking tickets (although those apply, as well). I'm talking about the blood, urine, and feces remaining after the body is removed from where it was found. The police don't do this.

Also, when people lose a loved one to suicide, they become more likely to make that choice for themselves. Suicide literally can become contagious. According to "Suicide Bereavement and Complicated Grief" from *Dialogues in Clinical Neuroscience*, "survivors of suicide loss are at a higher risk of developing major depression, post-traumatic stress disorder, and suicidal behaviors, as well as a prolonged form of grief called complicated grief. Added to the burden is the substantial stigma which can keep survivors away from much needed support and healing resources."[2]

Something to consider along with all the other unimaginable thoughts with which you are struggling.

If you think everyone may be better off without you, you are wrong. There is very likely no way to die gracefully by your own hand in this situation. Asking for help, talking to a friend, going to a safe place, and spending time in nature can all help to de-escalate your feelings when you are in crisis. Bringing your focus back to the present moment is an effective tool if you are anxious about the future. Although simple, a mantra that resonates can help calm a racing mind or heart. My favorite is: "In this moment, I have everything I need." I say it over and over until I return to calm. These things may sound silly to one in crisis, but sometimes the hardest thing to do is take that first step.

If someone you love comes to you with suicidal thoughts, be patient. Help them find help. Don't judge or guilt your loved one. They need support and care. Check in often. Sit quietly when necessary. Get help yourself so that you know how you can help and how you can care for your own mental well-being while walking this path with someone you love.

Another great resource on this topic is the book *Just a Normal Tuesday* by my friend Kim Turrisi. This novel is based on her experience with her sister's suicide and gives the reader a realistic picture of what this type of exit does to a family and one possible route to healing. A survivor support group is an invaluable tool for coping with this type of loss. You can search for a group near you at www.afsp.org.

THE BETTER WAY?

I struggled to come up with an example of a graceful exit by suicide by a person suffering mental illness. It's possible that there is no graceful way when hope for treatment remains. However, assisted suicide for the terminally ill is a different situation. There are so many emotions surrounding this topic that I recognize what I might deem graceful, others might find appalling. Ultimately, since death is so final in this physical realm and is not an exit between two people or a person and an organization, it is up to those who are exiting to define grace for themselves.

In January 2014, Brittany Maynard was diagnosed with a terminal and aggressive form of brain cancer called glioblastoma multiforme, the same cancer that killed Senators Ted Kennedy and John McCain, among others.

Just twenty-nine years old, Brittany was given between three and ten years to live. Shortly after her first surgery, her doctors discovered that her situation was worse than they had originally feared. She was then given just six months. Her family searched for alternatives and prayed for a misdiagnosis.

Brittany, however, was developing a different plan. When she realized that death from this particular disease would be especially brutal, she sought an alternative. She began to plan her death. She learned that the state in which she lived, California, did not have death-with-dignity laws, so she moved to Oregon to access that state's program for assisted death.

Brittany Maynard decided to go with dignity. She chose her death date and shared it with her family and friends. She was prescribed a drug that she could take at will, surrounded by her loved ones, to make her crossing peaceful and painless. Knowing this was an option brought great relief to her husband, Dan, who did not relish the thought of her suffering. This option also allowed Brittany and her family the opportunity to focus on spending quality time together with less fear of the unknown that would otherwise exist.

While all of this is remarkable and quite graceful, Brittany took her exit one step further. She went public. She announced her intentions to take her own life after encouragement from an acquaintance she met at a wedding. Her intention was to shine a light on what dying with dignity looks like and the hoops one must jump through in our country to be able to do it. The resulting media exposure was not something she sought but developed organically. The universe presented her with an opportunity, and she said yes. As a result, her legacy lives beyond her time on this earth, as her family fights to expand death-with-dignity laws to other states. As of the end of 2020, eight states and the District of Columbia have passed death-with-dignity laws. Brittany's family and the nonprofit Compassion & Choices continue to fight to expand these rights.

The beauty of this exit is breathtaking on so many levels. Brittany took care of her needs, which, in turn, took care of her family's needs and allowed them to honor her life and her final days in the best possible way. There were no surprises about what was coming. Brittany's choices also allowed her loved ones to keep her memory alive in a meaningful way. For more information about Brittany and her story, visit www.thebrittanyfund.org.[3]

PREVENTION

To be clear, I again say with love that there is no preventing death. However, we can prevent unnecessary stress and confusion when it comes to our own exits. With that in mind, perhaps it makes sense to plan for it using whatever means are available to us. There are plenty of services that can help you not only plan your funeral, but also prepay for it. Or you could just write instructions about what you would like, so no one is left to wonder—or, worse, to argue with family members about what they think you would have wanted. If you really don't care, write that down. The idea is to reduce stress for your loved ones once you are gone.

However, what if that hasn't happened and someone you love is inching closer to their ultimate exit? How do you ask about their wishes without sounding insensitive? The Conversation Project, created by Pulitzer Prize–winning writer Ellen Goodman, states as its purpose to "have every person's wishes for end-of-life care expressed and respected." Goodman started this nonprofit after her own mother passed without sharing her wishes for how she wanted to die. This organization is doing great work in helping to start the tough end-of-life conversation with those we love. Check out www.theconversationproject.org for conversation starter kits and tools for facing this difficult but inevitable transition.

In creating a graceful exit as one's time draws near, an important consideration is the energy of the space from which one will exit. A beautiful and peaceful environment is important to the dying, as evidenced by the common request to be at home as the transition approaches. Comfort and familiar surroundings are key. If being at home is not possible, do what you can to bring the feeling of home to the dying—wherever he or she is. Candles or diffusers can release familiar smells into the room, and favorite blankets and photos are reminders of home. In her book *Sacred Dying: Creating Rituals for Embracing the End of Life*, Megory Anderson suggests bringing "tools" into the picture. Tools are used to create a peaceful, soothing atmosphere that will help the dying person and all present to sense the divine presence. They tune into the senses and should be appropriate to the dying person's wishes and spiritual orientation. These are some general suggestions.

- Lighting: Soft lighting or burning candles can elicit feelings of peace and safety.
- Aromas: Burning sage, scented candles, or incense or the fragrance of fresh flowers can create a calming effect.
- Holy objects: Set up an altar and arrange spiritually meaningful articles or pictures on it.
- Music: Appropriate music soothes and inspires. Certain instruments of sound, such as drums or bells, are used in many traditions. Sounds of nature can be relaxing.
- Prayer: Oral prayer in keeping with the dying person's tradition, the recitation of psalms, or the reading of scripture may offer comfort. In Islam the Qur'an is read, and when the final moments arrive, there is complete silence.
- Silence: Always remember that silence is an important sound. It is good to remember the value and necessity of simply sitting in silence with the dying person.[4]

A great website, Dying Consciously (www.dyingconsciously.org), covers many aspects of making a graceful transition from this plane to the next. One of the posts I found pertinent concerns a Buddhist ritual: "When a Buddhist is approaching death, close friends and family members should sit with the dying person and help him or her feel calm and peaceful," the site states. "Death is a natural and inevitable part of the lifecycle, and the dying person should be made to accept this reality. Friends and family should help the dying person reflect on his or her good deeds in this life, and the power those good deeds will have over his or her next incarnation. A small statue of the Buddha may be placed by the head of the dying person and 'parittas,' or protective verses, may be chanted. More generally, the dying person should be made as comfortable as possible before death occurs."[5]

Once our loved one has departed, thoughts turn to grieving and our chosen rituals for coming together to honor the one who passed. When it comes to planning a funeral for someone we love, we often want it to be a celebration of life but fail to set that expectation clearly for our guests. In order to authentically change the mood at a funeral—or as my sister says, "put the fun back in funeral"—we need to firmly embrace the idea that it is okay to actually *rejoice*. No matter how much time the departed spent with us, no matter how he or she died, there is always much to celebrate. For those who were very young, we can share and celebrate our hopes and dreams for them, how they got their names, their favorite colors, songs, toys, etcetera. If they were older, we have a lifetime of experiences to share. Telling stories is the best way to keep the departed alive in our hearts. I have seen time and again how a grieving loved one's countenance shifts when asked to tell a story about a departed loved one. Weaving these stories into the service is one of the best ways to honor and celebrate a life.

Word of the time and place for funerals is often spread through friends of the family or on social media. This is a great time to get the message out about the desired tone of the service. Asking people to wear light-colored clothing often helps set a lighter mood. You can ask guests to share their favorite memories, sing, or speak to how the departed made an impact on their lives. Get creative! Display the memorabilia of the deceased. Were they an artist? Let's see it! Got any high school yearbooks? Bring those, too. Pictures? Yes—bring them all; each picture tells a story of a precious moment to be remembered. Video set to music is powerful and can be revisited time and again long after the service has ended. You can hand out DVDs of the video or post it on YouTube and let people know where to find it. This provides great comfort and is a lovely time capsule of sorts for future generations who may not remember or have met their departed relative.

At the funeral, the family of the departed sets the tone for the rest of the guests. If you are able, give permission to others to laugh by smiling and embracing guests or crying with joy if that is possible. There will be dark moments, for sure, because we all handle death in our own way. Yet when the celebration is done, wouldn't it be lovely to walk away with a feeling of joy after learning a few new stories about a loved one, along with overwhelming gratitude that we were lucky to know the person at all?

On the subject of grief, the work of Dr. Elisabeth Kubler-Ross cannot be overlooked. Her pioneering work around death and dying, developed from time spent with dying patients, resulted what we know today as the five stages of grief. She learned that the reactions of patients, when told they were dying, were similar to that of their families after they died. If you are new to loss or facing a terminal diagnosis, I highly recommend reading her groundbreaking book, *On Death and Dying*, as it serves as a roadmap in the strange land that is grief. Be kind to yourself and to those around you during this turbulent time. As she noted in *The Wheel of Life*: "When we have passed the tests we are sent to Earth to learn, we are allowed to graduate. We are allowed to shed our body, which imprisons our souls."[6]

On a personal note, when it is my time to exit, I hope that I can prepare my loved ones to embrace my transition with acceptance and joy for the life I have lived and my role in each of theirs. I have been known to throw a party or two; the coming together of loved ones brings me immeasurable joy. It is only natural, then, that for my celebration of life, I want just that: all of my loved ones together again sharing memories. Additionally, I'm a fan of the New Orleans jazz funeral, so that might be fun. Though I don't want to be buried, I love the idea of a marching band parading down the street, starting slow and sad, then moving into an upbeat tempo to which you just can't help dancing. At my celebration, I want massive amounts of hugging, dancing, peals of laughter, and heaps of love.

Since I prefer to be cremated, there would come a time when my sons would need to do something with my ashes. We've discussed this. They are going to put my ashes in a little wooden boat on their favorite body of water, shove me off, and light the boat on fire in a Viking-like ceremony. Beer, a bonfire, good food, and some stargazing will follow. What a send-off as I head into my next adventure! It is not goodbye, but bon voyage! I will be there, as well, in my new ethereal form, delighting in my greatest blessings.

THE BLUEBERRIES

You must know what blueberries mean by now, right? If not, that would indicate that "Un-humaning" is the first part of this book that you have read. For that, I am truly sorry as it suggests you are in a time of great pain. My wish for you is to find the beauty where you can and be kind to yourself. Also, "blueberries" represent the good stuff or key learnings from this chapter. You can find a wonderful story about this at the end of chapter 2.

- Introduce the concept of life span to your children. Pets are a wonderful way to do this.

- Face death as a part of life (the price of admission) and get comfortable with discussing it with others.
- Keep your relationships "clean." Do not let harsh words linger and make any amends necessary so that you can live with each conversation if it happens to be your last.
- When a loved one is dying, the only thing you must do is show up. The rest will fall into place.
- To ensure your own graceful exit, live the life of your dreams and make your wishes known.

Part V

EXCEPTIONS

Please know, dear readers, that you have been perched on my shoulder throughout the writing of this book. I have heard the occasional, "yeah, but what about . . ." or "what happens when . . ." or "easy for you to say." I understand that the examples provided in this book may not align as a perfect template that you can apply to your current situation. My intention is to start the conversation, help us build skill in a new area, and collectively improve upon this first step as we go. I also understand that there are situations so extreme that our definition of "graceful" must morph into an alternative outcome. This section is a starting point.

Chapter Eleven

Redefining Grace

Nature provides exceptions to every rule. —Margaret Fuller[1]

In some situations, a completely graceful exit is not within your control. Sometimes, it may be more important to get out quickly than to create a graceful exit for both parties. Knowing these situations in advance may provide the required clarity to take care of yourself first.

Sometimes, a sudden disruption occurs, and a person is ripped from your life without warning. Creating a graceful exit is not an option. However, even under these extreme circumstances, the "uncoupling" work can be done on your own through therapy, journaling, or writing letters that you never send. But first, let's go over a few examples in which grace is not the goal.

ABUSE

Sadly, there are many forms of abuse in this world. The very nature of abuse often precludes the type of graceful exit discussed in this book. If you are being emotionally or physically abused, it is imperative that you find a way to leave. Your *last* priority is trying to rationally talk through the transition plan with your abuser. Leaving in a manner that keeps you and those for whom you are responsible safe is the absolute top priority.

To accomplish this, you must develop a plan and find resources and assistance in advance and then execute that plan with extreme focus and commitment. Consider using someone else's phone or computer to research options so that your abuser cannot discover your activity. Contact your nearest domestic violence shelter, which will provide basic living needs and protection and help you and your children start a new life. Reach out to the National Domestic Violence Hotline at 1-800-799-7233 (SAFE) or, if you are outside the United States, the International Directory of Domestic Violence Agencies for assistance. There are several online resources and guides to help you.

Once you are safe, you can work on finding a place of spiritual grace in your heart for both yourself and your abuser. Seeking a counselor or therapist for this difficult but important work is highly recommended. Group therapy is another valuable option; there is such power in understanding that you are not alone. With time and patience, this effort will help you heal, forgive, break your patterns, and learn to trust again. This is where grace can be found.

In a relationship that includes substance or alcohol abuse, the dynamic is more confusing. The person you are with is not well and seems to more urgently need your help. However, if you have made the decision to leave and your partner is still using his or her substance of choice, a graceful exit in that moment is highly unlikely. Your focus must be on making your transition first and healing later. There are amazing organizations to help you deal with your experience, such as Al-Anon, Nar-Anon, and CODA. Reach out, seek guidance, and find others who have walked in your shoes.

If there are children involved, it is important to remember that children believe that they are half of each of their parents. If one parent says bad things about the other in front of the child, then the child feels that he or she is 50 percent bad. If the child hears both parents talking badly about each other, that kid is screwed. Biting your tongue might be the hardest thing you ever do, but it won't be harder than watching your child grow into an unhappy, self-loathing, or destructive human being. I beg you to do your best with this.

DISAPPEARING ACTS

Sadly enough, the most painful goodbyes are the ones that are left unsaid and never explained. —Jonathan Harnisch[2]

There are many examples of relationship "disappearing acts," in which someone chooses to disappear. For example, spouses run an errand and never come home—or run away with someone else. Partners break up with you via letter, text, or email, never to be seen again. Parents walk out before the child is even born. Free will means just that: we are not permanently tied to one another, no matter how badly one side wants to be. Other examples include parents who emotionally disown children for their life choices. It can also include loved ones lost to us emotionally because of a debilitating illness such as dementia or Alzheimer's disease.

Once again, in these situations, you must do the work on your own. Lady Deane, a dear friend of mine and fabulous psychic, astrologer, and medium, shared a lovely solution that was handed down from her grandmother. Here is what she shared.

Talking in the Ethers
Lady Deane

There are times in life when we need to communicate with loved ones but cannot because of separation. It really doesn't matter the cause of the separation—illness, absence, misadventure or, in some cases, even death. During these times, my grandmother had a method she called "talking in the ethers." As a child, I pictured the ethers as a sort of Neptunian mist, like an unseen aura or web of energy that connects us all, one to the other. Imagine my surprise, when later on, I discovered that one of Merriam-Webster's definitions of the ether was: "heavens" or "A medium that in the wave theory of light permeates all space and transmits transverse waves." Today, I suppose one might just call this "reaching beyond the veil." Whatever you call it, the method is pretty much the same. And, as with all intentional magic, it's the prep work that really counts. Being clear about your intention before you begin affects your success. Here's how it works.

First, before preparing your message, prepare your space. Create a divine or sacred space to work within. Clearing your space is always a good start and lighting a candle or burning a bit of sage or other herb should do nicely for that. Then, let's set the scene. Try to have a picture at hand of the person you hope to reach or communicate with. If you don't have a photo, then perhaps something of theirs that might have had some meaning to them will do—a favorite hat or book perhaps. If you have nothing that belonged to them, then play their favorite music in the background. Or maybe have something around that you would identify with them, such as their favorite color, flower, scent, etcetera. In other words, you're evoking them with your senses. Invite them into the room with you. It's only polite, after all. And even the deceased appreciate good manners.

Second, be aware that your voice has power. Whether you choose to write out your message ahead of time or speak it spontaneously, *say it out loud*. And best to speak from the heart—don't overthink it. This should be like a conversation; it should flow organically. In that sacred space, with your heart open, you will know what needs to be said. Trust that moment and trust your own voice. Then and only then will the air element carry the sound and meaning of your thoughts, feelings, and words into the ethers, where (according to my grandmother) delivery is immediate. Etheric messengers fly on winged feet and your words find their mark, living or deceased. Stay in the moment as this happens. You will feel the weight of your message leaving you, the burden of those words lifting.

Of course, whether or not you receive a reply is another matter entirely. Some will; some won't. Not really the point, though. In the end, all that any of us has is our own voice. Honor that, and your job is done. For what is left to be said if you have spoken from the deepest part of your heart? Be at peace.

On the other side of the equation, if you are the one planning to disappear—or already have—you carry baggage, as well. As long as you are alive and in possession of your mental faculties, there is still time to create a moment of grace. For example, what if you find out that your partner is pregnant with your child and you had no intention of ever being a parent?

If you cannot show up for that most important role, there are still things you can do, both to ease your own conscience as well as for the peace of mind of those you leave behind. You can write your child a letter in which you take full responsibility for your inability to be a parent and to assure the child that it has nothing to do with how wonderful and worthy he or she is. Take responsibility for your shortcomings and do not pass them along to your child. You can also pay your child support as mandated by law so that you don't pile the impact of diminished resources on top of abandonment. This is the least you can do for this life that you created. By doing so, you might give your child the smallest sense that your absence is not about him or her. It does not mean that the child is unworthy and has been abandoned because of any shortcomings. He or she is given the chance to see you as human and flawed, which is the truth. Without such communication, the child surely will think that something he or she lacks has caused your absence, which could not be further from the truth.

This is how you live with your own limitations without passing them on to others. In turn, you will sleep better at night.

If you choose to stay and be a parent, be the best parent that you can. Your child is your first responsibility, and it is important that you are as physically and emotionally present as you are able. Continuously try to improve in that role.

TRAGEDIES

When a loved one is taken suddenly through the violent actions of another or by a violent accident or tragedy, the concept of grace seems like sheer mockery. But stay with me. Beyond the horror, anger, and absolute anguish of those left behind, there is a tiny thread of opportunity that dangles before the loved ones. That thread is not seen or grasped by most, and that is understandable.

I imagine that the act of breathing would be difficult if one of my family members was taken by violence. I don't know that I could even write about this if I hadn't met a family that not only saw that thread, but grabbed it and pulled themselves through horror to find overwhelming beauty on the other side. I share their story as a beacon of hope for those breathing-challenged souls who are adrift in their own grief or someday might be.

I would like to introduce the King family.

Brent and Kelly King moved from Illinois to Poway, California, in 2008 with their two children, Chelsea and Tyler. They were a normal, happy family in a community of normal, happy families. Chelsea loved words, the French horn, and running. Tyler loved baseball and his big sister. Two years later, Chelsea, a member of the Poway High School Cross Country team, went for a run after school around a nearby lake but never came home. As word spread through the community that Chelsea was missing, hundreds and then thousands of people came forward to search for this vibrant young woman, including my own sister. While the search was ongoing, a suspect was discovered when his DNA matched a sample taken from a piece of Chelsea's clothing found discarded near the lake. He was arrested on suspicion of first-degree rape and murder. Tragically, Chelsea's body was found two days later.

What is so amazing about this incredibly sad story is the strength and grace exhibited by the King family. While their daughter was missing, they spoke to the media with hope for her safe return and gratitude for the community's outpouring of love and support. Even after the suspect was arrested and his past crimes revealed, they remained convinced their daughter had the strength to have survived. When the worst possible outcome was revealed, they showed up at Chelsea's candlelight vigil just six hours after her body was found to share their grief and thank their community.

The Kings did not stop there. They did not withdraw from that painful spotlight. Instead, they fought for hope and change. Within eight months of her passing, Chelsea's Law was signed into effect by then-California governor Jerry Brown. This law, driven by the King family and state lawmakers, ensures that violent offenders against children are no longer paroled but rather given mandatory life sentences. Because of this law, the more than nine million children in California are safer.

The Chelsea's Light Foundation was born in part as an effort to change the law in California but was expanded to help unique young people fulfill their dreams of going to college. The Sunflower Scholarship program selected local students who exhibited the same joy for life that Chelsea did and provided them with thousands of dollars for the college education Chelsea was never able to receive. Additionally, Chelsea's brother, Tyler, created a documentary about his sister's life and passing from his own unique perspective to raise awareness. This family gave meaning to tragedy in a manner that ensures Chelsea will be long remembered.

Forgiveness is often the gateway to grace when experiencing a death at the hands of another. Fatal car accidents happen, workplace accidents happen, and families are shattered as a result. Reaching a place of forgiveness is a steep climb but can make the difference between existing and truly living for survivors. I marvel at people like Mary Johnson-Roy who, in 1993 lost her son Laramiun at the hands of Oshea Israel after a fight at a party. Mary reached out to her son's killer twelve years into his prison sentence to ask if she could meet with him. From that meeting, true forgiveness was bestowed and a new relationship blossomed. Oshea became Mary's "spiritual son," and they remain active in each other's lives.[3]

If you are looking for additional resources about finding meaning in grief, David Kessler wrote a wonderful book titled *Finding Meaning: The Sixth Stage of Grief.* It is based on his own experiences of loss and his decades of work in the study of grief. The sixth stage is an addition to Elisabeth Kubler-Ross's five stages of grief, which focus on moving through the grief experience. Kessler adds the poignant and transformational next step of finding meaning and purpose after a loss.

This type of grace, under the most horrific of circumstances, exemplifies what to strive for when dealt such a blow. My friend Hayley lost her son to suicide, yet she bravely refuses to allow shame to taint his exit. She decorates his grave every Halloween (his favorite holiday) and invites friends and family to trick or treat there. She sends him messages on social media that ring true with the certainty that they will meet again. She does not allow him to be forgotten. This is her way of honoring him and what he means to her. While it may make others uncomfortable, she is doing her part to change the stigma and dialogue around his death.

Conclusion

Life is a comedy for those who think and a tragedy for those who feel. —Horace Walpole[1]

Grace is a choice. As Ralph Blum says, "more than we are doers we are deciders."[2]

Deciding to be graceful about an exit is an intentional choice that can make transitions easier on everyone. When you decide to exit gracefully, you can start by setting expectations from the beginning about how you will communicate with others if an exit becomes a reality. Exits, although difficult, are not to be feared; they happen throughout life. They consistently bring about the changes we need to become the humans we are meant to be. The more disruptive the exit, the higher the mountain we must climb to recover. By exiting gracefully, we spend less time crawling to the summit and more time appreciating the view and basking in the wisdom we have gained.

In the stories I have shared, there are commonalities among the ungraceful exits and among graceful exits. For any exit to be graceful, it should not be a surprise if at all possible. It should be made clear to all parties why the exit is happening, and time should be allowed for all parties to adjust to the idea of transition. It should happen with honor and respect for those involved, including yourself.

Of course, there are limits and exceptions for these guidelines, and perfection is not a realistic goal. Additionally, courage is required from all parties in both breaking and hearing the news. Exits require courage, honesty, and one's presence in the now to ensure there are no regrets later. We cannot control how others respond to an exit we initiate, but we can carry ourselves with dignity and integrity. And when we are the ones left behind—as we surely will be at some point—we can try to redirect our own reactions from anger, frustration, or despair to courage, understanding, and confidence that this is one of the many exits or transitions that make up a life. Letting go of what we think *should* happen and embracing what *is* happening is half the battle.

Finally, a graceful exit requires kindness. Put yourself in the shoes of others involved and communicate in a way that will allow them to best accept what is coming. Give others your time, even when you would rather be elsewhere, to help those you are leaving in their struggle to digest the transition. At a minimum, consider how you would like to be treated if the shoe was on the proverbial other foot and act accordingly. This can be accomplished in both business and personal relationships and should be the standard to which we aspire. And even if someone is not treating you the way that *you* would like to be treated during an exit, you can still strive to respond with honor, patience, and peace.

Better yet, do what you can to prevent painful exits by committing to the following: knowing yourself, loving yourself, and surrounding yourself with people who share your nonnegotiable values but who are also different enough to challenge you and help you to grow. Cherish moments as they occur so that you are left with no regrets.

It is not, my friends, the easier path, but it is most assuredly enveloped by grace.

Notes

PREFACE

1. Doyle, *Untamed*, 142.

INTRODUCTION

1. Goodman, *Boston Globe*.
2. Thomas, *Conscious Uncoupling*, 45.

PART I

1. www.goodreads.com/quotes/7322463.

CHAPTER ONE

1. Blue Mountain Arts Collection, *Love: The Words and Inspiration of Mother Teresa (Me-We)*.

CHAPTER TWO

1. Rock, *Your Brain at Work*, 140.
2. Kleinman, "Do Prenups Predict Divorce?"
3. Devee, "A Better Way to Break Up: Our Katherine Woodward Thomas Interview."
4. Unitarian Universalist Association, "Let's Talk about Divorce and Broken Relationships."
5. Unitarian Universalist Association. "Let's Talk about Divorce and Broken Relationships."
6. Thomas, "Calling in 'the One.'"
7. Atwood, *Be Your Own Dating Service*, 52.
8. Atwood, *Be Your Own Dating Service*, 53.
9. Atwood, *Be Your Own Dating Service*, 52.

CHAPTER THREE

1. Ferriss, *The 4-Hour Work Week.*

CHAPTER FOUR

1. US Bureau of Labor Statistics, "Annual Layoffs and Discharges Levels by Industry and Region," last updated March 10, 2022, www.bls.gov/news .release/jolts.t19.htm.
2. Cullen, "Remember Me."
3. National Safety Council, "Assault Fourth Leading Cause of Workplace Deaths," n.d., www.nsc.org/workplace/safety-topics/workplace-violence.
4. US Bureau of Labor Statistics, "Annual Layoffs and Discharges Levels by Industry and Region."
5. Laurence, "How to Conduct Mass Layoffs."
6. Robbins, "How to Conduct Layoffs."
7. Robbins, "How to Conduct Layoffs."
8. Sowell, "Fox News Called Him Socialist."

CHAPTER FIVE

1. Bonifant, "Empty Nest: When the Kids Leave Home, Who Is the Me Left Behind?"
2. Hendriksen, "Failure to Launch Syndrome."

CHAPTER SIX

1. Rowling, *Harry Potter and the Goblet of Fire.*
2. Bilski, "My Dad Lived a Lie."
3. Oliver, "The Summer Day."
4. Brown, *The Gifts of Imperfection*, 35.

CHAPTER SEVEN

1. *The Shawshank Redemption*, Castle Rock Entertainment, 1994.

PART IV

1. "A Message from Deepak Chopra," April 20, 2015, https://deathmakes lifepossible.com/a-message-from-deepak-chopra.

CHAPTER EIGHT

1. Travers, *How Lucky I Am.*

CHAPTER NINE

1. Keller, *We Bereaved.*
2. Kubler-Ross, *On Death and Dying.*
3. Plotz, "How Does a Hospice Nurse Work?"

CHAPTER TEN

1. Gibran, "The Prophet."
2. Young, Ilanit Tal et al., "Suicide Bereavement and Complicated Grief."
3. www.thebrittanyfund.org, https://youtu.be/uzp0tp8Fzio.
4. Anderson, *Sacred Dying.*
5. "Ceremony and Ritual."
6. Kubler-Ross, *The Wheel of Life.*

CHAPTER ELEVEN

1. Fuller, *Woman in the Nineteenth Century.*
2. Harnisch, *Freak.*
3. www.prisonfellowship.org/2015/07/a-mothers-forgiveness.

CONCLUSION

1. Walpole, *The Castle of Otranto.*
2. Blum, *Book of Runes*, 105.

Bibliography

Anderson, Mergory. *Sacred Dying: Creating Rituals for Embracing the End of Life*. New York: Da Capo Lifelong Books, 2003.

Atwood, Nina. *Be Your Own Dating Service: A Step-by-Step Guide to Finding and Maintaining Healthy Relationships*. New York: Holt, 1996.

Bilski, Jared. "My Dad Lived a Lie. I'm Determined My Kids Won't Have to Do the Same." *Washington Post*, July 12, 2018.

Blue Mountain Arts Collection. *Love: The Words and Inspiration of Mother Teresa (Me-We)*. Boulder, CO: Blue Mountain Arts, 2007.

Blum, Ralph. *The Book of Runes: A Compass for Navigating in Turbulent Times*. BetterLearn! E-books, 2012.

Bonifant, Susan. "Empty Nest: When the Kids Leave Home, Who Is the Me Left Behind?" Grownandflown.com. September 2, 2020.

Brown, Brené. *The Gifts of Imperfection*. Center City, MN: Hazelden, 2010.

"Ceremony and Ritual." *Dying Consciously: The Great Journey*. August 24, 2013. www.dyingconsciously.org/ceremony-and-ritual.

Cullen, Lisa Takeuchi. "Remember Me." *Time*, July 2, 2007.

Devee, Gina. "A Better Way to Break Up: Our Katherine Woodward Thomas Interview." *Divine Living Magazine*, May 2, 2017.

Doyle, Glennon. *Untamed*. New York: Dial Press, 2020.

Ferriss, Tim. *The 4-Hour Work Week*. New York: Crown, 2007.

Fuller, Margaret. *Woman in the Nineteenth Century*. New York: Dover Publications, 1999.

Gibran, Kahlil. *The Prophet*. New York: Knopf, 1923.

Goodman, Ellen. Ellen Goodman column. *Boston Globe*.

Harnisch, Jonathan. *Freak.* CreateSpace, 2016.

Hendriksen, Ellen. "Failure to Launch Syndrome." *Scientific American*, May 18, 2019.

Keller, Helen. *We Bereaved.* New York: Leslie Fulenwider, 1929.

Kleinman, Rachel. "Do Prenups Predict Divorce?" YourTango.com. October 4, 2012.

Kubler-Ross, Elisabeth. *On Death and Dying: What the Dying Have to Teach Doctors, Nurses, Clergy and Their Own Families.* New York: Scribner, 2019.

———. *The Wheel of Life: A Memoir of Living and Dying.* New York: Scribner, 1998.

Laurence, Bethany K. "How to Conduct Mass Layoffs." Nolo.com.

National Safety Council. "Assault Fourth Leading Cause of Workplace Deaths." Accessed March 14, 2020. www.nsc.org/workplace/safety-topics/workplace-violence.

Oliver, Mary. "The Summer Day." In *House of Light.* Boston: Beacon Press, 2012.

Plotz, David. "How Does a Hospice Nurse Work?" *Working* (podcast). November 20, 2014.

Robbins, Stever. "How to Conduct Layoffs." *Harvard Business Review*, March 2009.

Rock, David. *Your Brain at Work.* New York: Harper Business, 2020.

Rowling, J. K. *Harry Potter and the Goblet of Fire.* London: Bloomsbury, 2000.

Sowell, John. "Fox News Called Him Socialist." *Idaho Statesman*, April 15, 2021.

Thomas, Kathleen Woodward. "Calling in 'the One.'" YouTube. November 2, 2021. www.youtube.com/watch?v=KiSyRl_bbOA.

Thomas, Kathleen Woodward. *Conscious Uncoupling: 5 Steps to Living Happily Even After.* New York: Harmony Books, 2015.

Travers, Mary K. *How Lucky I Am—Winnie the Pooh Journal.* Cultural Bindings, 2017.

Unitarian Universalist Association. "Let's Talk about Divorce and Broken Relationships." www.uua.org. Undated.

US Bureau of Labor Statistics. "Annual Layoffs and Discharges Levels by Industry and Region." Updated March 10, 2022. www.bls.gov/news.release/jolts.t19.htm.

Walpole, Horace. *The Castle of Otranto.* Oxford: Oxford University Press, 2014.

Young, Ilanit Tal, Alana Iglewicz, Danielle Glorioso, Nicole Lanouette, Kathryn Seay, Manjusha Ilapakurti, and Sidney Zisook. "Suicide Bereavement and Complicated Grief." *Dialogues in Clinical Neuroscience* 14, no. 2 (June 2012): 177–86.

Index

About the Author

Geri Reid Suster has thirty years of experience in business and management, specializing in acquisitions and creating operational excellence. Between 2004 and 2006, Geri lost her mom, got divorced, started therapy, sold her house, bought a new one, and left her job as director of operations after eighteen years. After a year's sabbatical to recalibrate, Geri dove back into the corporate workplace, where she was promoted to chief operating officer. After jumping to a new technology startup that didn't pan out, Geri entered a period of reflection that led to an epiphany about "exits" that would change her life. In January 2017, as her two boys reached adulthood, she sold everything and bought a huge RV that she named Wallace (after William Wallace in *Braveheart*); the hashtag #whereswallace was born. In less than three years, she traveled to thirty-eight states in the United States and five provinces in Canada with her two dogs. In 2020, Geri sold Wallace, bought a Sprinter passenger van (named Wüfgang, #whereswüf), and built her own custom home on wheels with her nephew in eighty-one days. Still hooked on wandering, she spends most of her stationary time in Bend, Oregon.

CPSIA information can be obtained
at www.ICGtesting.com
Printed in the USA
LVHW111604121122
733002LV00003B/128

9 781538 169308